WE ARE THE WORK

Dick Bathrick

Order this book online at www.trafford.com
or email orders@trafford.com

Most Trafford titles are also available at major online book retailers.

Printed in the United States of America.

ISBN: 978-1-4907-2107-1 (sc)
ISBN: 978-1-4907-2106-4 (hc)
ISBN: 978-1-4907-2108-8 (e)

Library of Congress Control Number: 2013922582

Trafford rev. 01/24/2014

www.trafford.com
North America & international
toll-free: 1 888 232 4444 (USA & Canada)
fax: 812 355 4082

For Kathleen

CONTENTS

Foreword ix

Preface xi

Acknowledgements xix

Introduction xxiii

Chapter 1: Women's Voices: Central to the Work 1

Chapter 2: We Are the Work 27

Chapter 3: Community Accountability 47

Chapter 4: Organizing Men 77

Chapter 5: Race Matters: The Conundrums 89

Chapter 6: Times Changed and So Did We 111

Chapter 7: Intersectionality Matters: Connecting the Dots 133

Chapter 8: A Model for Change 141

Chapter 9: Patriarchal Violence 147

Chapter 10: Courage and Compassion 155

Epilogue: We Are the Work 165

Appendix A: The Core Principles 171

Appendix B: The Core Values of Because We Have Daughters® 177

Appendix C: How BWHD works 179

Appendix D: The Men Stopping Violence Community-
                        Accountability Model 183

Endnotes 185

About the Author 187

FOREWORD

"We Are the Work" provides a window not only on the development of Men Stopping Violence, but also on the history of the anti Domestic Violence movement in general. And it does so with vivid and instructive examples. I'm most impressed with Dick Bathrick's self-reflection and honest examination that portray working with men as a mutual enterprise of social/cultural change rather than a mechanical delivery of services. Both inner and outer work are essential. Bathrick also demonstrates the importance of seeking and listening for feedback and criticism—we never fully arrive and when we think we do, we haven't. The hard earned ongoing development of MSV is a story itself that brings out the bumps and human (and gender) struggles that often get pushed to the side. The writing is certainly clear and engaging—the narrative voice and straightforward examples make it so. I was also struck at how Bathrick managed to wrestle with many of the major issues in the work, ones that are still lingering—everything from the gender of group leaders, to the challenges of men holding men accountable, women holding men accountable, women in leadership, mobilizing men in general, and not just the ones who end up in a batterer's group. How violence against women is rooted in patriarchal violence, and what it takes to confront those forces. So I think the book has a special and important niche of program development and movement history. It brings a lot of unsaid or neglected sides of the work to the surface. But it also speaks to the reader personally in a way that prompts him or her to examine oneself along the way, reminding us that "We are the Work".

Ed Gondolf, author of "The Future of batterers programs: Reassessing evidenced-based practices"

PREFACE

In Memoriam

Kathleen Roach Carlin 1939-1996

Kathleen Roach Carlin was the Founding Executive Director of Men Stopping Violence in Atlanta and a national voice for many years in the battered women's movement. A native of Maywood, Nebraska, she received her BA and MSW degrees from the University of Nebraska. In the 1970's, she direct the Cobb County YWCA's Women's Resource and Rape Crisis Center and then help to found Men Stopping Violence. She also provided instrumental leadership in the National Coalition Against Domestic Violence and the National Woman Abuse Project during the 1980's. She was a teacher, writer, and visionary whose leadership in the work of making gender and racial justice made a significant impact on those with whom she lived and worked.

Kathleen Carlin died in 1996 at the age of 57 after a heroic battle with lung cancer. She taken from us long before she was ready to go and long before we were ready to let her go: she wasn't finished with us yet.

Kathleen was, above all, an unrelenting advocate for women. There were many ways in which she powerfully manifested her advocacy. As Founding Executive Director of Men Stopping Violence (date?) until her death in 1996, Kathleen modeled how women provide leadership and direction to men working to end violence against women and how men could work in solidarity with women within structures of clearly defined accountability. She expected much of the men who knew and worked with her. She expected men to boldly challenge patriarchy in ways that promoted safety and justice for women, while requiring accountability for men. She expected men to do their own work, hence the notion "we are the work." She also expected a lot from her women colleagues and friends. Solidarity was a given even as she would challenge our lazy, sloppy thinking or our hesitation to use our voices in the cause of justice for women. For those who got to experience her, these expectations were a gift.

When she was an undergraduate at the University of Nebraska, she was president of Chi Omega sorority where she learned the social graces of a young lady and at the same time, she was president of the student YWCA, where she learned about the need for justice and political organizing. This juxtaposition as a young woman perfectly describes who Kathleen was throughout her life; she put to use the skills she learned in both places. She was a woman of genuine elegance and a most gracious hostess who loved to welcome and entertain friends in her home, while at the same time, as a feminist, she carried an uncompromising social analysis which she was more than willing to share with anyone who would listen. This was not a contradiction in Kathleen; it was who she was. This combination served her well in her professional life.

After Kathleen returned to Atlanta in 1976, she pursued her work through the YWCA. Here she found a place where her Christian values and commitments to racial justice and to women could be supported. It was through the YWCA that she learned how important it was as a white woman to combat racism and she learned how to do that effectively. It was here that she began to work with and for battered women.

I used to tease her about showing up to speak or lead a training for what she knew would be a "challenging group" looking like a sweet, demure housewife from the suburbs, truly a "church-lady". Then she would open her mouth and out would come her unflinching radical feminism, challenging everything that we ever thought we believed; it was never empty rhetoric but thoughtful social critique of the patriarchy as we know it. The audience would listen because she had gotten past their defenses by her very presence. They didn't always agree but they had to listen. I affectionately referred to Kathleen as "the white lady from hell" because of her dogged insistence on the importance of confronting racism, heterosexism, and, for that matter, speaking truth to power whenever it was required.

She was a strong and fearless swimmer. I experienced this on our trip to the Philippines in 1994. We had a day at the beach and she and two other women from our group swam off at least 300 yards from the beach. When I looked up and saw how far out they were, I became anxious for their safety and called to them. After an hour, they made their way back in. One of the secrets to Kathleen's endurance at swimming was her ability as a great floater. She would lay back and totally relax, at peace in the deep water. She was definitely fearless and at ease in the midst of the deep water of advocating for women.

Kathleen was one of our intellectual pioneers. She was a remarkable teacher, trainer and lecturer. With her consummate ability to combine analogy, metaphor, humor and analysis, she would often stun audiences with her capacity to make terrible and complex truths clear and undeniable. Yet she did so with grace and strategic intent and never with hostility which allowed her to invite us into an awareness that then pushed us to action.

Kathleen's feminist analysis was unequivocal: men in our society use violence to control women and this pattern is sanctioned by the patriarchal institutions in which we all live. We will only end violence against women when we change the cultural norms which accept and reinforce male dominance over and control of women. She approached this task institutionally and individually through Men Stopping Violence. As the founding Executive Director, she helped to shape a program which intervenes directly with batterers, challenging their behavior and calling them to account. She also believed that this work with the men should be done by other men who are supervised by women. She asserted that it was men's work to confront other men but that it was necessary for women to monitor men's work in order to insure that it did not inadvertently cause further harm to women. The clarity of her thinking which was reflected in her teaching and writing was a constant challenge and guide to her colleagues.

Kathleen possessed a wisdom that came from living a full life --- and she lovingly shared it with us on occasion. She knew that for us as women, "knowing" is better than not knowing. She never shied away from "knowing" even when that knowing was very painful. She never hesitated to share her knowing with us and to listen to ours.

Often she shared her wisdom with humor which is one of the things that many of us will miss the most about Kathleen. Even during the last period of hospitalization, her humor was sharp: when I asked her how she was doing with all the tubes, and IV medications, she complained about how often they had to flush the tubes: she said "I've been flushed so many times that I feel like a toilet in a bus station." Her humor spoke volumes about the way life is and always conveyed genuine affection to the hearer in the midst of sometimes painful circumstances.

Kathleen's spirituality was rooted in her music and her Christian faith. She would be at choir practice even if she would be out town for the Sunday service because, as she said, she needed to sing. She would process her knowledge of the world through her knowledge of her faith. She looked there for solace and support and often found it.

The writer of Hebrews reminds us: ""Therefore since we are surrounded by so great a cloud of witnesses let us lay aside everything and run with perseverance the race that is set before us . . ." She had a deep and abiding reverence for those witnesses who have gone before us, especially in the civil rights movement and the women's movement, those who surround us still and who, I'm sure received Kathleen's spirit when it departed this world.

What she didn't fully realize is how she played that role for many of us. During Kathleen's illness, I was hiking in the old growth forest in the Pacific Northwest. I noticed the huge Douglas fir trees -- almost as big as the redwoods of California. Occasionally, either by storm or disease, one of the big trees would fall. As soon as this tree was laid to rest, seeds would land on it and begin to sprout. Seedlings would make their home there. And in some places you could see that now another huge tree had grown --- now standing upon the first huge tree that fell. I thought of Kathleen. With her passing, truly a huge tree fell among us. But her work, her teaching, her vision, her writing, her witness -- all laid a foundation for the next steps of our work. She left us with a strong base upon which to build.

Of course for Kathleen and for many of us who work for social change, we don't see a lot of immediate impact for our efforts. This is especially true in working to end domestic violence. And Kathleen struggled with this. But she understood what the writer of Hebrews meant: "Now faith is the assurance of things hoped for, the conviction of things not seen." Then after listing out the ancestors in the faith, the writer concludes: "All these died in faith without having received the promises, but from a distance they saw and greeted them. They confessed that they were strangers and foreigners on the earth, for people who speak in this way make it clear that they are seeking a homeland . . . and God is not ashamed to be called their God; indeed, God has prepared a city for them."

Kathleen died in faith without seeing the fruition of her efforts: a world in which men respect women, in which women and children are safe in their homes, in which women's voices are valued and our gifts are celebrated. But she never wavered in her belief that we as human beings are capable of living in just relationships.

As she struggled to understand her own illness and its meaning, we talked about hope and about Vaclav Havel's comment that "hope is not about believing we can change things, hope is about believing what we do matters." Actually Kathleen changed a lot of things but most importantly, what she did mattered very much.

She left a legacy for those whose lives she touched. Her contribution to the battered women's movement and all of our efforts to end oppression and make justice among us was major and still resonates today. In this book, Dick Bathrick offers us a testament to Kathleen's ability to see and name reality but also to rally colleagues and companions in the collective effort to make social change.

Thank you to Dick for recording this important history lest we forget those who have gone before us.

Rev. Dr. Marie M. Fortune

Founder and Senior Analyst, FaithTrust Institute

2013

ACKNOWLEDGEMENTS

Many thanks to the people—most of whom I've known well, some I wish I knew better—who inspired me to do "the work," including this book:

To Red Crowley and Howard Gadlin, whose thoughts about how the world turns are in my head when I need them . . . and when I don't.

To Sandra Barnhill and Libby Cates, who brought way more to me and MSV than they were ever asked, and who guided us through our most gut-wrenching moments. Not sure MSV would have made it without them.

To Loretta Ross and Beth Ritchie, women whose speaking truth to power said things I sometimes wasn't ready to hear—but always had to know.

To my friends John Alderson, Bill Taub, Britt Dean, Jeff Jacobson, and Andy Sheldon, who so often bring the joy of laughing with and at men . . . and the wisdom not to know better.

To my friends and co-conspirators Ed Gondolf, Marie Fortune, and Jean Douglas who go about their work with a combination of relentless grace and power that blows the mind.

To Debbie Lillard, Shelley Senterfitt, John Trammel, Juliana Koob, Asher Burk, Aparna Bhattacharyya, Yolo Akili, Chi Ying, Etiony Aldarondo, Greg Loughlin, Sara Totonchi, Ayonna Johnson, Andy Peck, Jeff Matsushita, Kirsten Rambo, Mike Freed, Khaatim S. El, young(er) allies who took what "this work" offers and ran—no, flew with it.

To Linda Bryant, Ann Stallard, Julia Perilla, Sherry Sutton, Wendy Lipshutz, and the late Robin Nash, whose commitment to community building has cultivated the firm ground on which we who seek justice make our stands.

To the MSV board who showed up when things were rolling but especially when we were getting rolled: Cynthia East, Robert Hahn, Mary Krueger, Althea Sumpter, Judy O'Brien, Rachel Ferencik, Stacey Dougan.

To my sister, Serafina Bathrick, whose treasuring of the unconscious has been a great gift to many, including me.

To Brendan Bathrick, who so artfully produced our MSV logo, as well as the cover of this book.

To Barbara Hart, Donna Medley, Debby Tucker, and the late Ellen Pence, implacable muses of our Battered Women's Movement.

To men in our movement on whom I've leaned over the years: Rus Funk, John Stoltenberg, Antonio Ramirez Hernandez, Paul Kivel, Craig Norberg Bohm, Rob Okun.

To MSV staff current and past, from Rich Vodde to Ramesh Kathanadhi and Lee Giordano, for whom this work is way more than a calling. And special thanks to Jane Branscomb Collier, who did everything administrative and beyond, including sweeping our figurative floors to keep MSV going.

To Phyllis Alesia Perry, my dear friend and editor, who insisted that I keep telling this story, when it seemed imperative, and when it seemed pointless. A wonderful writer in her own right, we met faithfully at Dr.

Bombay's where she deftly guided me back to my own voice without imposing her own.

To our son, Sam, his partner Korin and their dazzling friends for whom egalitarian relationships seem to be minimum expectations and from whom I draw tremendous hope.

And finally, to my partner, Jesse Harris Bathrick, who, when she isn't tending to her luscious gardens, finds ways to share what and who she knows with others, generating deep connections among extraordinary people, many of whom contributed to this work . . . and to the person I have become.

MEN STOPPING VIOLENCE

Mission Statement:

Men Stopping Violence is a national training institute that provides organizations, communities, and individuals with the knowledge and tools required to mobilize men to prevent violence against women and girls.

Philosophical Statement:

We look to the violence against women's movement to keep the reality of the problem and the vision of the solution before us. We believe that all forms of oppression are interconnected. Social justice work in the areas of race, class, gender, age, and sexual orientation are all critical to ending violence against women.

INTRODUCTION

In 1982, Gus Kaufman and I pursued a job interview with Kathleen Carlin, then executive director of the Cobb County (Georgia) YWCA Women's Resource Center, for the position of facilitator of her newly funded, court-mandated batterers' program. We were an unlikely combination. Gus was a Jew from Macon, Georgia. I was a New England WASP by way of Fairfield County, Connecticut. Kathleen was a Methodist from Maywood, Nebraska. Gus's dad was a progressive icon in the Southern Jewish community. Kathleen's dad was president of the First National Bank of Maywood. My dad voted for conservative Republican Barry Goldwater in 1964. Gus was a clinical psychologist. I was a marriage and family therapist. Kathleen was a social worker.

But while we came from different backgrounds and disciplines, we shared strong common interests. For one, we all arrived at that interview having been powerfully influenced by the social change movements of the 1960s and 1970s. Prior to and during her term as the executive director, Kathleen had been working diligently to carry out the YWCA imperative to eradicate racism. Gus and I had been active in the anti-war and civil rights movements. Both of us had recently moved to Atlanta from New England, Gus to return to his Southern roots and I to live and work in a completely new and unfamiliar territory. We knew each other because Gus had been in a relationship with Jesse Harris, the person with whom I am in a lifetime partnership.

While in New England, Gus had made a connection with the staff at Boston-based Emerge, one of this country's first batterers' intervention programs (BIP). Gus and I shared a commitment to finding work that would be both personally relevant and socially redeeming. It's hard to say whether we really had a clue about what we were getting ourselves into, but working with "violent men" to address their abuse of women seemed to meet our criteria.

As Gus and I talked about starting a group for men who batter women, we asked Susan May, then the executive director of the Council on Battered Women, whether she thought our work with batterers would be a problem. We had learned that women advocates were concerned about the motives of men who professed to want to do work that could be vital to the safety of women: Were men in it for the money or would we appropriate women's ideas and experiences to serve men's interests? Those concerns made sense to us, and Susan told us she would let us know if she experienced us, and our proposed work, as problematic.

She soon had us listening to hotline calls to get a better sense of the challenges facing battered women. The raw truths conveyed in those calls were riveting and heartbreaking, and I think listening in brought urgency to our efforts to start working with men. It was while we were facilitating our first batterers' group in Atlanta that we pursued the job interview with Kathleen.

When we scheduled the interview, Kathleen gave us an assignment. We were to read her article "Why Women First," which had recently been published in the feminist journal, *Aegis*. The first thing Kathleen asked us when we arrived for the interview, even before we sat down, was whether we had read that article. The last two interviewees hadn't, Kathleen added, and she had terminated their interviews—and their candidacies—right then and there. Gus and I assured her that we had read it and both of us breathed easier as we proceeded with the interview.

It was a long time before I had a better sense of the importance of our first few moments together. We didn't realize in that moment that Kathleen was establishing a standard of expectations that would define our working relationship for the next 14 years. That was the first of many times that seemingly mundane moments turned out to signal major turning points in the development of Men Stopping Violence (MSV), the organization we went on to establish under Kathleen's leadership.

These moments often required us to engage in the kind of self-reflection that ultimately defined Men Stopping Violence's vision and mission, and our core operating principles. In that initial interview with Kathleen, we thought we were merely there to get a job. For Kathleen, it was to see whether Gus and I could work effectively with her to make it safer for women by changing men. What we eventually discovered was that we were in the earliest stages of establishing our first core principle: women's voices and experiences must be central to our work.

Such stories are the foundation of this history. They reveal the essence of how we developed our seven core principles and became Men Stopping Violence.

Several times while writing this book, co-workers and colleagues asked, "So who are you writing this for?" Good question, because you want your voice to speak to the people you most want to read it. But the first question begets others: "Why are you writing the history of Men Stopping Violence?" So here's a run at those related questions.

As for the who and why question, first, I'm writing this for those who have been notably moved by their experiences with Men Stopping Violence over the past 30 years: our staff, board, community partners (locally, nationally, and internationally), families, loyal supporters. It's for the people we've educated and trained, for those that we've reached and for those we've not yet reached. Over three decades that's a lot of people whose lives have been jolted in positive and sometimes painful ways. This book will speak to the nature and outcome of those jolts.

I'm also writing this for people whom we have not directly touched, but who are curious about how progressive social change organizations form and thrive in a culture that readily resists changes in social systems: people in academic, faith, government, and business communities.

Men Stopping Violence is but one of many social justice nonprofit organizations whose mission is to do good while doing no harm. I believe that what makes MSV's history worth knowing is that her story is made up of, in part, singular moments when we faced significant or difficult challenges and reacted by hanging in instead of folding up. Men Stopping Violence is unique because of what we did in those moments—basically stayed engaged when there were no easy answers. Staying engaged is no small thing, because from the beginning of this endeavor the question has always been: Would men hang in there when women challenged us on men's pervasive and profound disrespect of women?

Early on in Men Stopping Violence's history, I often heard battered women's advocates say something like: "A man who batters a woman . . . he may apologize, feel some guilt, even go into a batterers' program, but he's not going to change. Once a batterer always a batterer." And I had no reason to doubt those assertions.

What did I know?

I was invested in being "politically correct," which, in the context of our work at MSV, meant doing what feminist activists thought was best for battered women. Then, over time, as feminist thinkers didn't always or even sometimes agree on what that meant, we at MSV had to sharpen our analysis both to reflect the broad spectrum of feminist thinking as well as our own experience in the trenches.

For example, referring to the message that batterers never change, I not only believed it, in my first public presentations I would say provocative things about men's choices to abuse women that would antagonize men and intrigue women. For example, I would say men batter women because we can get away with it, because it works for us and because it's what we learned about how to relate to women. My suggesting that men intentionally choose to abuse women, that they're not in fact "out of control," alarmed both men and women.

Then, as I gained more experience in listening to advocates and working with men, I didn't alter my thinking about men's intentions, but I shifted my take on the meaning of the statement, "batterers don't, or can't, change." On the one hand, there's more than a grain of truth to it; historically, there have been minimal meaningful consequences for men who batter and the burden to stop him has rested primarily on the person with the least power and resources to make him stop—the battered woman. Under those circumstances batterers are unlikely to change. On the other hand, when men are respectfully held accountable and required to take responsibility for their choices, past, present, and future, they can change. I learned that they can change because they experience the benefits of living in a relationship based on safety and equanimity rather than fear and control. And they can start and sustain that change when the community around them insists that men's mistreatment of women won't be tolerated.

Ultimately, we had to recognize that the impetus for the change process didn't reside primarily within their relationship, or even in him, but in the society that shapes the attitudes and beliefs that govern his actions, that inform him what is legitimate and what is not, acceptable and not. And we realized that if we were to influence real societal change, we had to shift our focus from fixing or changing individual men in a group setting to mobilizing those communities that most influence all men's choices. This book is about how MSV negotiated that change process, the mistakes and subsequent discoveries we made. It's about the twisting road we took in forming and driving our mission and it's about the remarkable people who have affected and been affected by that ride.

Our uniqueness was also marked by the presence of women in leadership who would boldly speak difficult truth to power, i.e., women who confronted men (including us) on our male privilege by pointing out the illegitimate ways by which we acquired our privilege. That strength was bolstered by the presence of men who learned to experience that truth-telling as opportunities to transform themselves and ultimately the culture that condones and promotes men's violence against women.

In the late 1970s and early 1980s, small groups of men began to mobilize and join the women-led movement to end violence against women. The sociopolitical climate in which the battered women's movement gained major momentum was powerfully influenced by the social justice movements that had simmered and exploded during preceding decades. These were major struggles, including the fight for human rights for men and women of color, women in general, gays and lesbians, for survivors of poverty and war, among others. They were struggles in which members of different marginalized groups would sometimes unite to confront their common oppressors—and, sometimes, succumb to the divide-and-conquer tactics of those same oppressors, fighting amongst themselves.

For the relatively few men who attended the biannual meetings of the National Coalition Against Domestic Violence, the voice and soul of the battered women's movement, it was alarming and enlightening to hear women tell the "herstories" of their brutal and widespread subjection to the wanton violence of men. The truth-telling was powerful, not only for its eloquence but for its stark revelations of the ways that race, gender, and class were used by men to both oppress and divide women in their efforts to unite against men's violence. So, for example, women of color not only had to deal with the sexism of their brothers of color, they had to deal with the racism of their white sisters. Lesbians had to deal not only with men's heterosexism but also with their sisters' homophobia. And queer women of color had to deal with . . . well, all of it.

As one of those first men's organizations to address women's oppression by men, Men Stopping Violence often struggled with questions that sought to clarify and define men's roles and responsibilities in the work to end male violence against women. How, in a sexist world, could men work in true solidarity with women? And how, in a historically white-led movement, would we address racism? Given that all forms of oppression reinforce the oppression of women, how would we address the ways in which these oppressions intersect?

This book is about how MSV went about answering these and other vital questions and how those answers ultimately became the Core Principles of our work. It traces the origins and implementations of those principles. This is not a document based on research and evaluation, one that measures the impact of intimate partner violence and the effectiveness of batterers' intervention programs (BIPs) in addressing it, but by tracking MSV's growth it does examine the strengths and limitations of BIPs and particularly the role a batterers' intervention program can play within the context of community-based strategies. And this is not my memoir but, in effect, a memoir of MSV. It's how I remember MSV's inception and evolution, told in a narrative form that tracks the stories and events that shaped our work from 1982 to 2012. Sometimes I reference myself as an example of those who have been impacted by this work. Like many of the men referred to in this book who have struggled to come to terms with their role in either furthering or ending gender oppression, I've had to struggle with my own challenges.

For those who do this work it can be deeply personal and for those for whom the personal is political, it can get dicey. Maybe the people who last longest and keep bringing themselves fully to the work are those who have found and cultivated a profound appreciation for the absurd. And maybe I'm just talking about myself.

I've tried to identify not just the "usual suspects" who have contributed to our work, but also some unique characters who have participated in some unexpected ways.

MSV's history is packed with teachable moments, some from which we learned and grew, some from which we didn't. I hope there will be enough of both to make this an intriguing read.

CHAPTER 1

Women's Voices: Central to the Work

I'm a woman who speaks in a voice and I must be heard
At times I can be quite difficult, but I'll bow to no man's word
We who believe in freedom cannot rest.

"Ella's Song," Bernice Johnson Reagon,
Sweet Honey in the Rock

One of the interesting ironies in the work to end male violence against women is that many of the men who come to it do so believing that if we just work and try hard enough we can avoid making mistakes that might make us look bad in the eyes of women or, for that matter, other men.

That belief reminds me of my earliest days of learning to become a family therapist, when I would attend workshops by the master clinicians in the family therapy world. Often they would present video excerpts of their therapy sessions with terribly difficult families in which they would invariably do dazzling work. Families would transform before our eyes. Those of us in the audience would applaud enthusiastically while quietly questioning whether we could ever measure up.

Then one day Gus Napier, one of the family therapy gurus of his time, intentionally showed a tape in which he took some risks with a family that didn't turn out well at all. And suddenly, those of us mostly novice therapists in the room became incredibly energized as we talked about his choices and what he could have done differently, or what we would have done differently in his place. The room was electric with learning.

No One Way

The lessons we learned that day mirror some of the more important ones we incorporated in our learning process over the years at MSV. One is that there is no "one way" to do this work. And when you do this work you will experience many moments when the answers aren't easy and often unknown. This work requires creative and bold risk-taking that sometimes results in incredible breakthroughs—and sometimes in painful mistakes. And—this is very important—in those mistakes lie amazing opportunities for individual and organizational growth. So often it was the mistakes we made that required us to stop and formulate the core principles that would guide our practice.

I can't recall when it was that I came to understand that making mistakes was an inevitable part of doing the work of confronting male hegemony. So much of that work was counterintuitive to the way I saw and did things. More often than not women had the unenviable task of pointing out our blind spots. So this book is also about the lessons learned when women brought difficult truths to me and other men and what we did when that happened. These struggles to we had as men to tune in to women's reality helped solidify our Core Principle, **"Women's Voices Must Be Central to the Work."**

Good Intentions

In 1982, Gus Kaufman and I were conducting a Wednesday night court-mandated class for batterers in the Powder Springs Library in Cobb County, Georgia. Two months into the six-month class, we began noting the leadership qualities of one of the men in our class, who was doing an exceptional job of keeping all of the contractual agreements: he had attended all the classes, arrived early, paid his fees punctually, participated actively by giving other men in class strong but caring feedback, and by consistently claiming the details of his abuse towards his partner in the incident that resulted in his being referred to our class. In short, he was emerging as the hands-down class leader, and both Gus and I were pleased to acknowledge his positive influence to him and to his classmates.

Kathleen Carlin and Leigh Ann Peterson were supervising our work at the time, and we provided detailed descriptions of each man's performance in the room. Leigh Ann was the staff liaison to the female partners of the men in our class.

When, in the second month, Gus and I began to dwell on the leadership qualities of the man I will refer to here as "Ted," Leigh Ann made a special effort to reach out to his partner, whom I'll refer to here as "Mary." After two weeks of failed attempts to reach Mary on the phone, Leigh Ann made a home visit to see how Ted's partner was, in actuality, faring. It turned out that the reason Leigh Ann couldn't reach Mary on the phone was because Ted had discontinued phone service to the house. He had also required Mary to quit her job, had taken away the keys to her car and had forbidden her to have any "unauthorized" contact with her family or friends. Mary was, in effect, being held hostage in her home by the man whom Gus and I had anointed the "star" of our class.

The supervision session following Leigh Ann's home visit with Mary was grim for Gus and me. It was the beginning of the end of our illusion that we could reliably determine how well a man was progressing in class based on his performance in that class. It was the beginning of our realization that the way to accurately assess how well men in class were progressing was to hear from the liaison/advocates truths about how men were treating their partners at home. And not just the court-referred batterers in the class. When Kathleen and Leigh Ann began to require us to provide audiotaped recordings of our work in class, they could give us concrete examples of when we were either establishing and maintaining a climate of accountability in the room and when we were consciously or unconsciously colluding with the men.

I recall several occasions during those revelatory supervision sessions when Gus and I would learn a very unsettling truth about how our choices would or could result in putting a battered woman more at risk. And I would just go silent and numb in the room. I couldn't really think or feel a thing. I'd just fix my gaze on the rug in Kathleen's office and wait for some kind of thought or feeling to return. Gus would excuse himself and, by his report, head for a stall in the men's room where he would wait out head-splitting sinus attacks. After we'd "collected" ourselves, we'd rejoin Kathleen and Leigh Ann and the rattling work of righting our wrongs.

We were beginning to learn, painfully, that our well-meaning efforts were not enough. As the old proverb says, the road to hell is paved with good intentions.

Sometimes during those intense meetings with Kathleen and Leigh Ann, when Gus would unwittingly say or do something sexist I would think to myself, "Damn, I'm glad I didn't say that." Looking back at that now, I wonder under what conditions does it become as uncool to say sexist things as it is to do or say racist things. In the early 80s, just like today, men felt free to say sexist things and expect other men to join in the laugh—often in the presence of women.

Today beer ads are notorious for presenting men as feeling more attached to their beer, feeling freer to describe their feelings of love and loyalty to their brew, than to their girlfriend. And then, when she reacts in dismay or disgust, he looks at us as if to say, "What's her problem? I was just playing."

So what does it mean that while there's been a slow but seismic shift in men's consciousness regarding sexism, Anheuser-Busch still makes millions of dollars selling men mocking women? And in that same genre of beer ads, we are also seeing a woman bartender refusing to pour beer for a guy because he's carrying a purse, introducing the apparently lucrative connection between sexism and homophobia. I think of these beer ads as barometers of the extent to which corporate sponsors feel free to use sexism and homophobia to promote products to men. Hard to imagine these sponsors seeing racist humor as profitable. Not that racism is any less alive and any less crippling in its effects. It's just that the public in general, and media moguls in particular, know better than to make blatant attempts to profit from racism.

I think that in the early 80s, Gus and I were struggling with how to create the kind of tipping point among men where it would become as unacceptable to say and do anything blatantly sexist as it was to be blatantly racist. But we were clearly knee deep in our efforts to deal with our own sexism, which brings me back to those intense supervision meetings with Kathleen and Leigh Ann.

There was one particular incident in which I tellingly revealed my unexamined sexism. Kathleen had requested that I submit a monthly written report on our work with the men in our group. I remember the stunned look on Kathleen's face when I handed her several somewhat rumpled pages of notes with cross-outs and scribbles in the margin. And then she handed it back to me, saying something like "You'll need to present this in a readable form." I recall Leigh Ann either saying or looking like she was saying, "What were you thinking?" It was, no doubt, occurring to all four of us that my report revealed my tremendous lack of respect for her position as my supervisor. And I'm sure that Gus, too, was wondering, "What is he thinking?" It was flagrant enough for us both to revisit the question we would ask ourselves and other men who do this work: "So are we that different from the men with whom we work in our groups?"

While it was clear that Kathleen and Leigh Ann were distressed by these discoveries, they seemed to know that making mistakes was inevitable in this work and were often more understanding of us than we were of ourselves. Later in the car ride home, Gus and I would laugh at the weird ways we had acted in the room, but I think we knew that our bodies were responding to the serious consequences of our well-intended efforts in the best way they knew.

Setting the Bar

Nonetheless, given the choice of looking to women for feedback or relying on our own experience or judgment, Gus and I still instinctively looked to our selves as the experts on men. After all, conventional wisdom told us that men know men best. On the other hand, analysis of how oppression works tells us that members of subordinated groups have to know the dominant group, and be experts on them, just to survive. Just as slaves on the plantation had to know the master's every move and mood in order to survive safely, women have learned the importance of studying and knowing men's tendencies in order to avoid men's rage. And so, in the course of our supervision by Kathleen and Leigh Ann, we began to hear things about their experience of men, including ourselves, that were disturbingly insightful.

Take, for example, the decision to audio-record our classes with men. After the "Ted" debacle, Kathleen and Leigh Ann decided that they needed a clearer picture of how we did our work, so they decided that we would tell the men at the beginning of the group that we were being supervised by two women's advocates who required us to record the class.

As we sat down to begin the class, I sincerely believed that once the men heard that we were being supervised by women who "required" us to be accountable for our work, they would, in disgust for our acquiescing to women, vehemently protest, and or just get up and walk out. So I read my opening statement, which I had carefully written out so that I wouldn't forget or minimize the message, turned on the recorder, and waited for all hell to break lose.

But nothing happened. The men just went ahead and began the class as usual, one by one introducing themselves and acknowledging whether or not that had used controlling behaviors on their partners during the preceding week.

I was amazed. For one, the men didn't appear to have much difficulty with the idea that two women were supervising us. And second, if they weren't having difficulty with it then it probably meant that I was the one having difficulty with it; I was the one experiencing resistance to the idea that women had the right and the knowledge to tell me and Gus how to work with men. I think that what I was also struggling to understand then was that Kathleen and Leigh Ann were much more focused on the obstacles and anxieties of the women who weren't in the room than on the needs and challenges of the men who were in the room. Therefore, their expectations of those men, and, for that matter, of Gus and me, were high. I, on the other hand, and particularly in the early days, was caught up with the importance of "joining" with the men in order to gain their trust and ultimately their confidence in our program and me. My thinking was that once you earned their confidence you could then require more of them. I was pretty sure Kathleen and Leigh Ann didn't understand the importance of that. Over time I grew to understand that it wasn't an either/or proposition, that in fact one of the best ways to gain the respect and confidence of men who came to us to "change" was to expect a lot of them from the very outset: set the bar of expectations for men early and set it high and men will rise to that level. And when we began with low expectations of men and set the bar low, men would go low.

When Kathleen and Leigh Ann matter-of-factly expected me to tell the men that women were requiring the recording, I was, in effect, telling them that the priority in the room was the safety of the women who were not in the room. I had to shift my stance to one where I expected men to bond around the primary needs of women. And when I did that and men responded positively, I discovered that by making women's needs a priority could actually be experienced by men as being in men's interest.

Kathleen and Leigh Ann understood that. That understanding was difficult for Gus and me to hold on to. Without the weekly supervision we couldn't see when we were compromising that. Our first challenge was to do something that we were asked to do that really didn't make sense to us, go ahead and do it anyway, and then have the unnerving experience of knowing that they were right. But if Kathleen and Leigh Ann had not been in position power to require that, Gus and I, whenever we felt uncomfortably challenged, could have easily agreed to disagree with them and proceeded with our own ideas of how to work with men.

Because Men Must

Our supervision experience was providing us with the tools to understand the meaning of women's reality so that we could consistently bring it into the room. But why wouldn't we solve the issue of how to bring women's truth into the room by simply making women co-facilitators in the room? Many batterers' programs were already doing that, so why wouldn't we?

Kathleen had strong opinions about that, which she laid out in her article "Working With Batterers: What is Women's Role?" In it she presented compelling reasons for her insistence that men co-facilitating classes. Incidentally, none of her reasons suggested than women were unprepared or unqualified to work effectively with men. In fact, she stated early in the article that many women want to be in the room precisely so that men can hear directly from women what it is to be the object of their violence and abuse and, because they have co-facilitator authority in the room, so that they are less likely to be ignored or discounted.

Kathleen built her case for male co-facilitators in the article by naming the goals of a batterers' program:

> "What is the task, ultimately, of a batterers' intervention class? Ultimately, that task is the undoing of sexism. . . . The premise that is often stated is that a man learns to be violent from his family—either from abuse that was perpetuated against him or that he observed. While this is true as far as it goes, it misses the more profound basis for his violence: a sexist culture, which is then played out in families. Our belief is that men learn primarily from other men to be violent, so that's where they have to unlearn it. Therefore, the batterers' intervention class should simulate the sexist society, not the family. A group co-led by a man and a woman tends to suggest the family, with the facilitators subconsciously representing husband and wife or mother and father, further suggesting that the violence is of concern only within the confines of the family—in other words a private matter."[1]

And, to further explain her preference for having male facilitators in the room, Kathleen spoke to the conditions under which men "get real" with each other:

> "It seems likely to me that when a woman is in the room with a group of batterers, some version of

10

chivalry will kick in, meaning that men won't 'get real.'
Possibly the batterers will behave in the ways they are
supposed to behave with "good women" (in this case,
women with authority in their lives). But it's how men
talk about women when women aren't in the room that
counts. If men don't talk directly about their contempt
for women, get challenged, have to take responsibility
for it, they won't change."[2]

So, since women are contending with men's misogyny day in and
day out, Kathleen took the position that at Men Stopping Violence the
men would take primary responsibility for confronting it. Not because
women can't, but because men must.

Kathleen also contended that when men in the room struggle
with their homophobia, their fear of reaching out to other men when
they are confused and vulnerable, it will serve women and men better
to have men taking on the responsibility of taking emotional care of
one another:

"Because men confiding and showing feelings of
sadness and fear to other men risk being seen as
weak (like a woman) or of becoming emotionally
close (homophobic anxieties), men usually talk with
women in their lives about their feelings. Therefore,
in a society that is highly homophobic, men (and
women) will be more comfortable having men talk
about their feelings if there is a woman in the room.
A woman facilitator who will necessarily respond to
men's emotional expression will, unwittingly, ease the
(men's and women's) homophobic anxiety in the room

when, instead, men must confront their homophobia if they are really going to confront their contempt for women."[3]

So, if women weren't going to be in the room bringing women's perspective on the work as co-facilitators, where would they be? What would the structural relationship between men and women doing the work look like?

We had been grappling with these difficult decisions since our first encounters with Kathleen and Leigh Ann, and it would take time and some more difficult lessons learned before we came up with viable answers. Kathleen had a way of providing "teachable moments" that would inform our decision-making process. These teachable moments often required us to look at the social context in which important decisions were to be made. And one of the ways that she would explore the importance of social context would be to invoke the metaphor of "leveling the playing field." For example, when she would speak to the meaning of hierarchical relationships, Kathleen would describe the way that oppression of any kind is based on the premise that the social "playing field" is tilted in such a way to favor the interests of dominant social groups—whites, heterosexuals, men, etc. And when you apply justice-making tactics (for example, by challenging an individual racist act) to a field that is already tilted to favor the privileged, regardless of the efficacy of the tactic, if you don't address the unlevel playing field the outcome will inevitably remain unlevel and unjust.

One of those "teachable moments" took place when, in the first two years of our work, a group of pro-feminist men decided to set up a study group to deepen our understanding of feminist theory and to support the work we were doing with men in our classes. We soon realized that we needed guidance or direction from feminist women regarding what readings we might select and how we might conduct our discussions in a way that was consistent with feminist process. One of us approached Kathleen, asking her if she would help us form and then facilitate our reading group discussions. She said she'd get back to us and when she did she agreed to facilitate our group discussions at a rate of $50 per hour. I remember feeling distinctly taken aback, not so much by the proposed amount but by the mere fact that she was going to charge us anything at all. And I wasn't alone. I think the unspoken, shared assumption of us men was that Kathleen would want to voluntarily encourage and support our efforts. But by charging a fee Kathleen was holding up a mirror to one of the fundamental but invisible tenets of male—female relationships: Women are there to support and encourage us in seeking our dreams and achieving our goals. It's understood and expected that women are here to do this for men, but not so assumed that men are to do this for women. By charging the fee Kathleen was exposing the tilt in the field and saying that women's assumed support of men has been historically unseen and undervalued, that men value the meaning of money, and that when we pay for her consultation we are demonstrating that we value that work and that we will respect the authority that she brings with it.

Kathleen would, at other times, emphatically point out that she and other women in the movement were not there to support men's work. That, on the contrary, we (men) were there to support the justice-making work of women who were about leveling the playing field for all women.

As a footnote to the study group experience, Kathleen eventually established a rotating system of paid women consultants for the group. And, on at least one occasion, even with the authority established by the fee and the role of consultant, we pro-feminist men, using verbal and physical intimidation, challenged the thinking of a lesbian consultant, to the point where she excused herself, citing her unwillingness to submit herself to that level of disrespect. We (men) then went about the work of taking responsibility for our abusive behavior, but it wasn't long after that that we learned from the women consultants that their humiliating experiences weren't worth the money we were paying them.

Through these early experiences, including her supervision experiences with Gus and me and the study group, Kathleen was formulating principles and circumstances under which women might work with men doing gender justice work. At the time I thought these experiences and the lessons we learned from them were specifically applicable to the work we were doing in and around Atlanta. Kathleen was having other thoughts.

In 1982 the National Coalition Against Domestic Violence invited Kathleen to address a special institute on "Working With the Abuser." At the time this was controversial since there were strong concerns that allocating attention to work with abusers would inevitably deplete the already limited resources available to the battered women's movement. Before an audience of some 300 mostly women's advocates from across the country, Kathleen presented a radical blueprint for how men could work with women to address male violence.

In her initial remarks, she made a point of noting her social location as a white, middle-class, heterosexual woman who wouldn't be speaking for all women and who would welcome the voices and perspectives of women of color and other marginalized women in the room. In a historic, fascinating, 45-minute address, Kathleen spelled out the conditions under which men could work with women without replicating the exploitation that has historically characterized those "working" relationships.

First, speaking to the issue of the cultural assignment for women to be the caretakers of men, Kathleen addressed how challenging it is for men and women to undo those roles and to experience women's power and authority as key to the outcome of the work. In explicating that challenge, she made the case that if men are to engage in unfamiliar, if not unnatural, acts to stop men's oppression of women, men will have to turn to the experience of women to know when they are furthering safety for women and when they are undermining it.

After Kathleen spoke I remember thinking that while these concepts were to instruct men, she was also speaking to women for whom these concepts could be equally challenging because patriarchal values are as internalized by women as they are by men. And by feminists as well as all women. With hindsight I can also say that eventually women of color took up her invitation and challenged some of her assumptions regarding how and why women of color would establish their leadership in relation to men of color in ways that are different from how white women established their working relationships with white men. Those challenges resulted in some of the changes we came to incorporate in our analyses and practice that will be addressed in a subsequent chapter about the Core Principle **"Race Matters."**

And so, leaning heavily into principles of anti-racist work she learned from Dorothy Height, the YWCA's founding Director of Racial Justice, Kathleen was proposing a model "in which men dedicated to anti-sexism work with men would (sic) deal with their fundamental issues of power over and rage toward women but with this work being done under the leadership and control of the women in the battered women's movement. Women who know that rage and abuse towards them and can point it out. So again, this is a model of having those who oppress taking responsibility for that oppression and for changing it, all the while acknowledging that only those who are victims of it can finally say what and where that oppression is."[4]

Over the next few years, Kathleen would refine this notion of women "monitoring" men's work, the foundation of which she introduced in this speech when she outlined the following behaviors that would be required for men to work in true solidarity with women:

Listening. First she highlighted the importance of men learning to listen and take seriously women's perceptions and realities of their experiences of men. I later understood that she wasn't suggesting that men had to agree with everything women saw or said, but that we had to focus more on taking in their difficult truths—with compassion and without judgment. We would not need to suspend our critical thinking, but rather just check our rush to judgment and refrain from the kind of "white-knuckle" listening in which we would focus on anticipating and preparing our responses rather than taking in information. As I heard this I was again reminded of the sometimes agonizing hours of supervision Gus and I had spent with Kathleen and Leigh Ann.

Valuing. Second, she recommended that we experience women's monitoring of men's work as having value, being valuable work, and that we compensate it accordingly. Here, she may have been drawing, in part, on her experience with our study group and the importance of women getting appropriately compensated for the value of their work.

Trusting. Another behavioral requirement was trust. Essentially, Kathleen was proposing that women working with men would have to be able to trust men to the extent that they could honestly and directly tell men when they didn't trust them and why. Here's how she put it: "To be able to say, with safety, to someone who has more power than I, 'I don't trust you,' requires a fairly high level of trust."[5] She then referred to how unsafe it can be for a battered woman to acknowledge to her abuser in a therapy session that she doesn't trust him because he may very well turn on her then or later for telling the truth.

Sometime later as I was thinking about the trust thing, I thought about Art Foster. I met Art when I was directing a youth program on the south side of Chicago in the late '60s. Art had recently completed a 15-year sentence in Joliet State Prison for strong-armed robbery. He was volunteering with us and was terrific with kids, especially gang youth.

Not long after we hired Art, he acknowledged that he didn't know if he could trust me because I was a white, middle-class guy who didn't know the streets and he'd never trusted any white person before. I guess I could have gone to the place of wondering where Art got off distrusting me when he's the one who got nailed for a felony. But I realized that he was taking a big risk in being real with me, his supervisor with white privilege and the position power to fire him.

So we agreed that we would work to find out what it would mean for us both to demonstrate that we were trustworthy, because it wouldn't have served either of us well for me to go to white liberal guilt and fail to hold him accountable because of his having been oppressed as a black man from the streets.

In that light it made a lot of sense that Kathleen would propose a model in which women could directly acknowledge their distrust of men as a step towards establishing trust.

Waiting. The final behavioral requirement was to for men to wait, noting that women have historically waited for men to come home from work, from war, from watching or playing sports.

Kathleen was focusing on how important it is for women not to get into this working relationship until women are ready. This would inevitably mean that sometimes men would have to wait—while women deliberated, decided, changed their minds, and then decided again. And since men perceive waiting as passive and what women do, this would be no small requirement. Kathleen completed her address with a final challenge to the women and the men in the room:

> "These are some thoughts that I hope point us toward
> the exquisitely complicated and difficult qualities
> of this issue. Because what we are talking about is
> addressing the most profoundly significant difference
> in the human species: the difference between men and
> women. And so we come back to the primary question:
> What do we do with the difference? Do we fight it
> and attempt to dominate and control it, which is our

history, or do we engage it, and allow it to nurture our being whole?"[6]

The response was thunderous. And, as I stood there applauding with the rest of the room, I felt somewhat stunned. I no longer saw her as the executive director of the Cobb YWCA Women's Resource Center. It was the beginning of my seeing her as a major force in a very powerful battered women's movement. I knew this speech would have implications for Gus and me and a lot of other men. I just didn't know what those would be.

Men as "Experts"

One of the things that Gus and I noticed during the earliest days was how quickly and readily people adopted us as domestic violence experts. It seemed within days of our deciding to do the work that we were getting requests for interviews from the media. Our understanding of "domestic violence," what there was of it, was mostly derived from reading and listening to battered women's advocates. And I can remember on a number of occasions feeling like an imposter. For example, often when there was an incident in which a woman was beaten, stalked or sexually assaulted by a man, we were called by a reporter to weigh in with our opinion or to give "the man's side of the story." We would talk with each other about whether or not we'd participate in the interview and, if so, what we might say. And, because most of our ideas weren't original and were born from feminist writings, we would ultimately say some of the same things women were saying. But because men were saying them, the words were given greater validity and importance. It was an interesting dilemma that played out frequently over the years. We knew that we shouldn't—and really couldn't—speak for women, but we could also see how we could reach men who wouldn't ordinarily give credence to women's opinions. And I suspect it was often maddening for women to witness men taking seriously ideas that had been labeled "strident" or "man-hating" when delivered by women.

Eventually Gus and I learned the importance of crediting our sources, but sometimes we didn't give credit because we would either "forget" or maybe we would just *think* that we had thought of the ideas ourselves. Then Kathleen and other women would challenge us on our privilege: the privilege to speak women's thoughts without being subjected to woman-hating responses, and the privilege to forget whether the ideas were original or borrowed.

This imposter feeling surfaced in a variety of ways. I can remember being invited to go on the Atlanta-based Reverend Ike's morning radio show to talk about men's perspective on domestic violence. Reverend Ike was a forerunner of the prosperity preachers in the Atlanta African-American talk show community. Reverend Ike would ask us questions about what made men do these things and what was women's part in the whole thing. Of course what wasn't being discussed was the meaning of a white guy like me pontificating on this subject to a predominately African-American audience. And it was hard to know if Reverend Ike cared one way or the other.

At that time, in the early '80s, I believe Gus and I were trying to figure out whether, in the absence of men's voices speaking up about men's violence against women, it was better to have a white male voice speaking up from a feminist perspective rather than no male voice at all. Already, given our awareness of racism and its powerful connection to sexism, we were becoming clear about the importance of reaching out to men of color to join us in the work. At one point, Bill Engram, an African-American who was doing batterers' groups for The House of Ruth in Baltimore who agreed to consult with Men Stopping Violence, was very direct in his advice to us. It was specifically in reference to the fact that we were conducting a two-hour court class for men referred from bond hearings in which more than 95 percent of the participants were men of color and the men facilitating the class at that time were white. I was hoping he would say, "You need to stop conducting that class until you have men of color to teach it," because I questioned the efficacy of my teaching that class. Instead he was emphatic in saying that given that those men had no other place where they could struggle with the difficult truths around men's violence against women, and that the women of color in their lives needed them to wrestle with the questions we put to them, we needed both to continue teaching the class and to double our efforts to recruit men of color to facilitate it. It reminded me a little of when Kathleen told us to audio record the men's class in Cobb County. I did it because I trusted that the person telling me to do it knew more than I did about the meaning of it, not because it made sense to me. And, in both cases, I did it even though I felt unprepared to do so.

It's interesting to think about why there was so much energy around establishing us as "experts." Was it because there was a conspicuous absence of men's opinions on why so many men violate women? Or was it because there was already a growing resistance to hearing women talking about men's pervasive violence against women? If the latter were true, then the interest in hearing the "other" or the men's side of the story was born out of a need for a "come-to-Jesus moment" where men would stand up for men and tell the truth about how women provoke and abuse men. Whatever the reasons were, we were feeling the need to be able to effectively articulate our position on why men batter and what it takes for them to stop. At that time we were still very invested in seeing batterers' groups as the solution, which led to our pursuing training on how to facilitate batterers' groups and how to work with women advocates while doing that.

Women in Leadership: From Theory to Practice

Early in 1983, Gus and I attended an Emerge training in Ashland, Massachusetts, where we experienced pro-feminist men teaching women and men how to work with batterers. Founded in 1977, Boston-based Emerge was the first abuser education program in the United States.

Though they now have women in major leadership roles, when we encountered them in Ashland they were a men's collective. David Adams, who led the training at Ashland and who has been in a leadership role with them for thirty-six years, remembers how their collective relied on achieving consensus to make their decisions. Their process was slow and deliberate in an attempt, I thought, to address some of the power dynamics which men engage in when making decisions within a hierarchical framework.

It was in the spirit of searching for our identities as group leaders and apparent experts on working with batterers that we arrived at the Emerge training: ruminating on our own working relationship and hungry to hone our abilities to work with men. I remember during introductions on the first morning of the training a man stood up and self-identified as a batterer, describing in detail what he had done to abuse his wife. I recall thinking this guy was either brave or crazy to reveal these things in front of total strangers, a significant number of whom were women.

The response from the Emerge staff was that since he hadn't done any work to address his abuse, and since there were survivors in the room, it was inappropriate, if not abusive, for him to disclose this information without first checking with the presenters. He was also required to leave the conference immediately. While I experienced this event as somewhat awkward, it was one of the first times I witnessed a man being held publicly accountable by other men. I noticed that Emerge treated this man with respect while holding him accountable. I also realized that I hadn't even thought about how women, and particularly survivors, would be affected by his disclosure. I was mostly focusing on whether he was being brave or crazy. And I remember wondering again how I was going to acquire the awareness of the importance of women's experiences when trying to figure out how to work with men.

One way to grow that awareness was for us to pay attention to the voices of the women at the training, and one of those women was Pat Merchant, a strong women's advocate from

Richmond, Virginia. Her voice became a source of understanding and inspiration. Gus and I quickly gravitated towards her, in part because of her brilliance, and in part because of her spectacular sense of humor.

Pat came to the conference as the Director of a YWCA Women's Center for survivors of rape and battering. Prior to that she had served as a priest at a Richmond Episcopal church, where she also decided to end an emotionally abusive relationship with her first husband. As a result, she was fired by the church's rector who, as it turns out, was in the midst of having an affair himself. At the Women's Center, Pat became increasingly aware of the extraordinary courage and resourcefulness of survivors, as well as the myriad of tactics that men employ to control women.

So Pat came to the Ashland conference because she was powerfully drawn to the idea of men holding men accountable. She recalls experiencing the men at the conference as willing to risk being real with each other in the presence of women: "I just hadn't met men in the church or any place who were so radically honest about their controlling behaviors, even the more subtle ones like emotional withholding." Emotional withholding, of course, is one of men's most effective tactics for keeping women confused and off balance. When it's "working," a man will abruptly shut down emotionally for any or no apparent reason, leaving his partner and others wondering what she's done wrong and what she needs to do to make things right. Since information is power, the withholding of thoughts and feelings can instantly establish a power imbalance in which the withholder benefits from his partner's often futile attempts to pursue information that will provide clarity and reduce tension. Pat noted emotional withholding because it was a part of the Emerge teachings on the "continuum of male violence against women." Like the Duluth Power and Control Wheel, it demonstrated how male violence is more systematic and intentional, and less a matter of choices that are random and out of control. The Emerge training was important because we got to experience a collective of men educating a group of men and women on how to intervene with batterers. Connecting with Pat was huge, because it led to further work with her.

Within the year Gus was invited to keynote in Richmond on the role of men on ending men's violence. While there we connected with Marie Fortune, who was also keynoting and who, eventually, would team with Pat, Kathleen, Gus and me to provide powerful faith-based presentations in Atlanta and beyond. Ashland also revealed to Gus and me the need to increase the number of men in Atlanta who might take up the work with batterers. We knew we weren't ready to conduct such training, but, in addition to Emerge, we were reading the work of Raven in St. Louis and the Domestic Abuse Project (DAP) in Minneapolis. We concluded that, since the work of DAP in Minneapolis was directed by Mary Pat Brygger, their woman-led work might best reflect our work with Kathleen. In June of 1984 we hosted a two-day training at the Martin Luther King Center, facilitated by Mary Pat and her male staff. By all accounts the training was successful, particularly in establishing Men Stopping Violence as the local authority on working with violent men. Following the training Kathleen invited Mary Pat to consult with the three of us on how we might proceed in setting up a non-profit organization, specifically, what our three roles would look like. Looking back on it now, Gus and I speculate that Kathleen and Mary Pat had spent some time thinking about this prior to our meeting because it didn't take that long for us to conclude that it would make most sense for Kathleen to become the executive director of Men Stopping Violence.

Since Kathleen's presentation at the Milwaukee NCADV Conference in 1982, the three of us had been talking about how to incorporate the principal of women monitoring and taking a leadership role in men's work with batterers. Asking Kathleen to assume the role of executive director would put her in a position of power that would be congruent with that principle and it would reflect real and not token authority over our work. Gus would assume the role of clinical director, since we were still espousing a group-therapy model for working with men at that time. I took the title of community relations director since we had prioritized strengthening our relationships with community partners. It all made a kind of practical sense, but I know I was wondering how the community would react to a woman being "in charge" of men's work with men. Or was I really wondering how *I* would react to it?

CHAPTER 2

We Are the Work

If you wanna make the world a better place
take a look at yourself and then make a change.

"Man in the Mirror," Michael Jackson

Gus and I were already experiencing our own struggles regarding decision-making during that period. We were invested in sharing the responsibilities and the power that came with the work. But we were young men who were new to each other and unfamiliar with how to make joint decisions. In fact, one of the first important decisions we made was to decide to do things jointly. That meant, for example, we would co-present and co-facilitate using the co-facilitation of our group to demonstrate how men can share leadership and responsibilities equitably. We were very intentional about rotating the responsibility of collecting fees, welcoming men in the room, leading exercises, and confronting men on their abuse. In that regard, we took turns being the person who would say the difficult things to a man who had broken contractual agreements, whether it was by re-abusing his partner or by failing to participate fully in the group. We would take turns being the "tough cop" or the "good cop" since most men, when confronted directly, needed a voice of encouragement to resist withdrawing or lapsing into blaming their partner or into their own guilt or shame. In those days a term like "tough cop" made sense since we probably thought of ourselves as often enforcing accountability rather than facilitating the process of men holding other men accountable.

But even with our good intentions we had our struggles. We struggled over issues such as: who was bringing the most men into the group, who was generating the most income, and who was to be our spokesperson when one was called for. Gus was the oldest son of four children, with an older sister and a younger sister and a brother. I was the third of four with an older sister and brother. Even though Gus was younger by three years, I experienced him as saying and doing things more freely and authoritatively than me. And that was great, because he moved us quickly to make decisions, for example, coming up with the name "Men Stopping Violence," as well as with our first organizational brochure. I was more likely to monitor and bring up conflicts that would arise between us.

You could say that we were carrying out our birth order roles and it was mostly working well for us. But when we got stuck and realized we needed help, we reached out to Bruce Pemberton, a psychologist and the co-founder of the Men's Experience, a consciousness-raising support group for men, and a respected mentor to many men in the Atlanta community. Bruce volunteered to supervise us, and while that didn't resolve all our issues, he was vital to our getting them on the table. By requiring us to look at our own attitudes and beliefs about money, keeping agreements, and male privilege, particularly as they applied to our own relationship, Bruce was helping us figure out how to challenge men in our group about how they used money, failed to keep agreements, or used male privilege to control their partners. It was hard but invaluable work.

Our intentionality around sharing responsibilities represented some of our earliest attempts to form our organizational culture. Our supervision experiences with Kathleen and Leigh Ann had already revealed the importance of establishing the centrality of women's voices in all areas of our work. Now, as we were trying to figure out how to teach abusive men how not to be, we also had to figure out alternatives to those behaviors, or how *to be*. Gus and I decided to try to model less traditional ways that men could relate to each other and to confront some of the destructive ways men relate to each other—ways rooted in, among other things, being controlling, being judgmental, and being "right." Eventually, we decided that since we had received the same socialization around how to be men as the men in our groups, it made sense for us to "check in" with the other men in our group. Checking in was the way we required men to take responsibility for their sexist behaviors by claiming the specific controlling behaviors they had used during the previous week. We wondered if it would undermine our authority to reveal the ways that we were more like than unlike the men in the group. But more often than not the men expressed appreciation for our willingness to share our own mistakes. They would admire our willingness to be "real" with them. It was also true that sometimes men would say, "Well if you guys, the so called experts, are still doing these things, how do you expect us to change?"

It became an opportunity for us to remind the men that confronting male privilege, male violence, and the sexism in which it is rooted is lifelong work for any of us who decide to do it. The decision to check in with the men in our group signified that we recognized that we, or anyone doing this work, would need to deal with our own sexist attitudes, beliefs and practices, if we were to be able to honestly and with integrity, confront other men on theirs. In that sense, we understood that their change process was integrally linked to our own. It's why we subsequently required that all male candidates for our staff, as well as interns, go through our 24-week program for abusers. In later years, when we were intentionally describing our organizational culture by giving labels to the Core Principles of our work, we coined the term, **"We Are the Work**," meaning we men who do this work, have to undergo the kind of rigorous self-scrutiny that we require of the men in our classes. How could we require them to claim their mistreatment of women if we hadn't claimed our own?

Beyond Basic Training

Without claiming our own sexist behaviors, sooner or later our denial and minimization of our own sexism would result in our denying and minimizing theirs. To get to the root causes of my sexism I had to identify my key teachers and the take-home lessons they taught me. It meant that I needed to take a closer look at my "basic training" on how I got socialized as a man.

To stay with that military metaphor, I had to ask myself who my drill instructors were and what bottom-line messages I had to master if I were to "pass muster" as a man. Looking at it now, I can clearly see the training grounds and how there was a kind of consistency to the message and the method. And that while, over time, the instructors would change, the messages would remain relatively consistent.

As a child I dutifully noted, watching dads, brothers, uncles, and men in general carrying out traditional male roles, including that of men as the providers and the protectors; they are responsible for putting the food on our table, the clothes on our backs, the security in our home. As "head of the household," they had final say and ultimate authority over most matters. I don't know that my dad actually did all these things, but I understood that he was *supposed* to do all these things. And if or when he didn't, it got interesting. For example, when my dad had a stroke in his early 60s, he was hospitalized and unable to manage the family finances. My mom, who heretofore had never, as far as I knew, ever balanced a checkbook, suddenly had to manage the money. And she did it, very effectively. But when my dad recovered and decided to take back the finances, suddenly she reverted back to not knowing or caring about the numbers. Even though my mom was the everyday sergeant-at-arms, meting out jobs and discipline in our house, when things got testy she would invariably invoke the classic, "wait until your father gets home."

I believe that in households where the dad wasn't present, for whatever reason, the mom was still saddled with the task of promoting and enforcing patriarchal principles. For example, even if she were the primary or sole head of the household, she would promote the principle that a man is the appropriate head of a household. There were also less explicit corollaries. In the delegation of responsibilities, the mom was to oversee all things relational, gauging the emotional climate of the family and ensuring that the individual and collective emotional needs were met. If someone was dazed or confused it was on her to notice it and to fix it. She would arrange the social life of the family, facilitating social functions interactions within and without the family. And if there were conflicts, it was understood that she was ultimately responsible for finding a solution. There was also a lot of emphasis on the importance of women's appearance: looking thin and pretty.

So in the early years of my "basic training," I learned that men were the deciders with ultimate authority over all family matters. Their male privilege meant that they could decide if or when they would take on home responsibilities like childcare, discipline, and household chores. Their frequent silence or absence meant that when they did speak or "show up" it had a special meaning. And, while there might have been mystery surrounding what they were thinking or feeling, or where their work might take them, there was no confusion when they spoke with a raised hand or voice. Women were there to reinforce all this and to look good while doing it.

No one ever told me this. I just watched and took it all in. Meanwhile, I was getting complementary "basic training" messages at school. When I hit my middle and junior high school years, my most memorable teachers were guys who were just a little older than I was. They set the pace around how to look, what to wear, how to walk (there was what was called a "varsity" walk which incorporated a little hitch in your step to signify a possible sports injury), and how to talk, particularly to girls. These lessons took place in specific places where boys would typically congregate to tell stories, places like the bus stop, the back of the school bus, the playground, the locker room. These were the places where guys would talk and tell stories that would describe what it would take to be "cool." Puberty had kicked in and our voices, our bodies and our thinking were changing. Strength was big. To feel and to look strong was incredibly important.

And I was noticing that in our school the Italian guys were maturing faster than others of us, including me. They seemed older, faster, wiser, and stronger. They had muscles and hair in the right places. They were among the guys at the bus stop and on the playground that had stories—about girls—that were gripping. They seemed to know exactly what girls were like and what girls liked, how to get one, how to treat one and, by their account, girls were looking for "take charge" guys, guys who "wore the pants."

If you weren't "in charge," there were terms for you: terms like "punk," "pussy," "wimp," or "faggot," that essentially compared you to girls or guys who were like girls. So the worst thing a boy could be or be like was a girl or gay. I've since come to understand how the mere labeling of boys in those terms was the beginning of my being taught to feel contempt for girls and gays. It didn't mean I didn't like or want to date girls. It just meant that I wouldn't want to be anything like a girl or to possess any qualities that would be associated with a girl. And, god forbid, would I ever admit to feeling like or caring for a gay person.

The playground was one of the early testing grounds for boys, where there were standard rituals for proving your "manhood." The following scenario was typical of this kind of "test": Sometime or times you might find yourself called out by a group of boys to "stand up and fight." You didn't necessarily know why they were coming for you. You may have done something to provoke them. But you may have done nothing and it was just your time to prove yourself. You knew the drill; when backed up against the playground wall you were challenged to fight or live with the consequences of refusing to fight. Those consequences included merciless name-calling, as well as the understanding that if you didn't fight right then and there, they'd be back for you the next day, until you did. Somebody had to win and somebody had to lose. I remember that there were some guys, either because they were incredibly brave or totally terrified that would walk away, and face the consequences. Today we might use the term "bullying" to describe this ritual. Back then it was considered an unspoken and common "code of conduct."

But my "basic training" wasn't all bad. It was mixed. My sports experiences with football, basketball, and rugby exposed me to coaches and other men who extolled the virtues of hyper-masculinity. While I sometimes questioned the sanity of the men around me screaming obscenities and woman-bashing insults, comparing me and my efforts to women and their genitalia, I loved the intense competition and camaraderie. And sometimes I excelled, at one point becoming the captain of my college rugby team. I wasn't thinking much about the messages I was absorbing along the way. Messages like "no pain, no gain," "suck it up," "when the going gets tough, the tough get going," "do or die," "winning isn't everything, it's the only thing." But when I think about it now, one reason I was good was that I learned to administer and absorb physical punishment without concern for injury, mine or others'. And I would use sarcasm, mocking my own injuries, to inspire a sense of physical sacrifice while discouraging anyone's acknowledgement of emotional or physical fear or pain. I knew that these messages worked to win games. I had no idea or concern about what it would cost me in my abilities to relate to women and to other men.

For me, as much as I learned to love and depend on women, I know the strategies employed on athletic fields and courts further reinforced my conflicted feelings for women and especially those qualities permitted in women that were unequivocally "unmanly," such as the capacity to openly feel and express fear, pain, doubt, and vulnerability, the ability to feel and express empathy for another. As a man you were simply not going to win a game, a job, a woman, or a war if you were stumbling around trying to figure out what others were feeling. These experiences on the playground and on playing fields taught me some basics around manhood and strength that I would later re-examine to understand myself and other men—and some of which I would have to unlearn in order to pursue and sustain meaningful relationships.

When I would facilitate the Men Stopping Violence orientation for potential candidates for the 24-week batterers' program, I would routinely refer to the playground basic training ritual to illustrate how our male socialization sets us up to mistreat women. I noticed that the majority of men in the room, no matter what their age or ethnicity, knew exactly what I was talking about. They knew all the name-calling terms (though, over time, they would add new ones like "soft" and "bitch"). They were completely familiar with the playground manhood test, frequently offering their own stories of how they survived it.

It was important in that orientation to connect the dots between what we learned on the playground and how that influenced how we would handle conflict later in life when we found ourselves in primary relationships. I would suggest that combining the message that we were to wear the pants or be considered less than men, with the take-home message from the playground test, you fight or you fail—the outcome resulting in a winner and a loser—represents the most complete body of preparation that most men bring to relationships regarding how to negotiate a power struggle. Where or when, besides the home and the playground, does a man learn how to resolve conflict and negotiate differences, fairly and peacefully in an intimate partner relationship? Was there ever a course that a man could take either in elementary school, high school or college that could prepare him to do one of the hardest things ever required of him: to be a true partner in a primary relationship?

He either saw it modeled effectively by his parents or he relied on OJT (on the job training), resorting to seat-of-the-pants strategies steeped in playground nuance. It's ironic that one of the few places a man can learn how to negotiate challenging differences with an intimate partner only becomes available after he has been identified as a batterer and enrolls in a program.

The redeeming message in all this is that these attitudes and beliefs are learned and that just as we learned distorted messages around strength and masculinity from preachers of the patriarchy, we can unlearn them and replace them with messages that affirm ours and others' humanity. And it's important to note that while most of us young men were exposed to these messages, many of us chose not to adhere to them. Many of us chose to embrace notions of strength that uphold moral, intellectual, spiritual, and aesthetic excellence, notions that said you could be powerful without being overpowering.

"We are the work" is the ongoing practice of deconstructing the messages we've learned about what it means to be a man, espousing the ones that allow us to be in loving relationships with women and other men, confronting the ones that demean and degrade others simply because they fail to meet the standards required by "basic training" for men.

One important caveat regarding the principle, "we are the work:" Kathleen once described the men at MSV as "defectors from the patriarchy." I have often wondered about that because my understanding of the meaning of "defection," defined in the Oxford Dictionary, underscores "the abandonment of one's country or cause; ceasing in allegiance to a leader, party, religion or duty." There is, in this definition, the implication that defection is irrevocable or irreversible, as in "once a traitor, always a traitor," so that once you've abandoned your cause there is no turning or coming back.

But when your "cause" is patriarchy, there seems to be an exception to the rule of the irrevocable. And, among pro-feminist men, I believe we know that no matter what we might say or do to discredit or disown patriarchy, we will always be welcomed back in the ranks.

I first learned this in my sophomore year in college just after I had joined a fraternity. I joined because I liked the guys and wanted a place to party. During the "rush" period I went through an experience in which the "brothers" were screening potential candidates for the "house." The way it worked was the president would slide-project photographs of the faces of freshman candidates on the living room wall of the fraternity house. Sitting in the dark the brothers would rate the candidates by either labeling them as "hot," using terms such as "face man," "jock," or "stud." Or "cold," using terms such as "sofa," "lamp" or "rug," meaning that the candidate qualified as "furniture" or someone you wanted in the room to fill in the décor, but whom you wanted no part of as a "brother."

That was the culmination of several disturbing moments as a new brother, which resulted in my deciding to quit the fraternity. When I officially informed the fraternity that I was no longer a member and the reasons why, an interesting thing happened: I wasn't shunned. On the contrary, I was invited to give it time and to think about it. And, even though I never changed my position, I continued to be welcomed in that and every other fraternity on campus. Despite informing the national office of my decision and the reasons why, I continue, to this day, to receive newsletters updating me on fraternity happenings.

I learned that no matter what I might do to renounce my place in the "brotherhood," I could, at any moment, "belly up to the bar" with the boys, be welcomed with open arms, and resume all the privileges of its membership. I think that when Kathleen talked about defectors from the patriarchy, there was an unspoken notion that as defectors we were irrevocably banished from the "table," that there were steep consequences for making such a choice. But I've long thought of those consequences as being minimal, if not fleeting, at best.

"We are the work" is also about willingly revisiting our complicated relationships with patriarchy and our privileged location within it.

Gus and I noticed that the decision to put ourselves on the continuum with all men who control women ignited some unanticipated challenges for us—and for Kathleen. We would often say that we were more like than unlike the men in our classes. We demonstrated that "likeness" in ways that were particularly challenging for Kathleen. For example, two of our group facilitators were suspended and ultimately fired because of their drug and alcohol abuse. Two other staff members were put on probation for having abused their partners. One man on staff, in apparent defiance of the MSV policy to not do couples work until a man has completed the program and his partner has indicated that she feels safe to be direct and honest with him, disqualified himself by providing couples work for one of the men in his group while he was still in the group because, according to his clinical judgment, it was safe to do so.

All of these men had gone through our internship and it was ultimately Kathleen's responsibility to impose the consequences. Meanwhile, most battered women's advocates wanted, if not needed, to see us (the men who work with batterers) as leaders and experts who were different from batterers because we hadn't or wouldn't do abusive things to women. In that paradigm, we were the "good" men and batterers were the "bad" men. It made women uneasy when we would say things like "there are no good men or bad men, there are just men," because if they couldn't trust us to be different, who could they trust? And were we actually telling them that we were no different from batterers?

Kathleen saw the meaning in this and didn't want us to trivialize the devastating effects of batterers and battering. She would say that of course the men at Men Stopping Violence commit abusive acts towards women. The difference is that those acts were not committed as part of a systematic campaign to dominate women and that men doing this work are committed to stopping their abuse by taking responsibility for that behavior and by participating in an accountability process that will discourage them from using those behaviors in the future.

Accountability Groups are the Work

When advocates told Gus and me to stop checking in with the rest of the men in class, it was because they felt we were taking up valuable time. We complied, but we were left in a quandary. We knew that one reason we were effective in challenging men on their controlling behaviors was because we had spent years scrutinizing our own. And we weren't just going through the motions when we checked in. We had acquired the habit of being accountable and had experienced the benefits of monitoring and reducing our sexist beliefs and behaviors. So we were uneasy about what would happen if we didn't participate in that weekly structured check-in. That uneasiness had been expressed by many men who, as they readied to leave our

24-week program, would wonder aloud whether they could "make it" (meaning remain violence-free) without the group, and particularly without the weekly check-in.

Our solution was to set up an accountability group for men on staff (including interns) to come together on a bi-weekly basis to check in on our use of controlling behaviors at home, in our workplace, and in the rest of our lived lives. Our check-in process mirrored most of the requirements of the men in our classes: review a controlling behaviors checklist, claim what you had done, how others were affected and what you were going to do to address that behavior. We would then give each other feedback. Men could also request time to talk about issues that may have contributed to their controlling behaviors.

To increase transparency and accountability, we audio-recorded our meetings and made the recordings available to the women on our staff, giving them the choice of whether or not to listen to the tapes and provide us with feedback.

Meanwhile, in accordance with our organizational mission, we were finding ourselves challenged to confront not just sexism, but other forms of oppression as well. For example, we were often dealing with racism in our classes, sometimes because a man might reveal his racism while describing something he had said or done during the week, or it might surface as a result of the way a man might treat another man or other men in the class. We would invite men to explore the function and effect of their racism just as we challenged them to deconstruct their sexism.

Once again, as in our preparation to respectfully challenge men's sexism, we realized that our staff, specifically white men and women, had to intentionally address our individual and collective racism. We realized that since we said and did things that marginalized people of color, we would have to address racism in ourselves if we were going to effectively address racism in our classes and in our trainings. We subsequently formed a white people's accountability group that was attended by white men and women on our staff. We operated from the understanding that just as it was men's responsibility to address sexism when it surfaced in a room, it was white people's responsibility to confront racism. Not because women or people of color couldn't do it, but because it was time for men and white people to use the privilege of their social location to take it on. The ways that sexism and racism mutually reinforce each other and the way that society tacitly and explicitly condones white privilege led us to conclude that we had to put a major focus on racism in our work. That focus resulted in the formulation of another of our Core Principles, which will be discussed in more detail in a later chapter, **"Race Matters."**

As we became increasingly aware of the deep connections among the various forms of oppression, we could no longer minimize the importance of confronting heterosexism, as it was manifested by men in our classes and, of course, by those of us on staff. So, as we had done with sexism and racism, we set up an accountability group for straight men and women on staff to deal with our heterosexism.

But it's telling that it took years for us to overcome our resistance to addressing heterosexism. Some of that resistance was rooted in our having established an unofficial hierarchy of oppressions in which sexism and men's violence against women merited more attention, because addressing racism and or homophobia would distract us from our true mission. The rarely spoken assumption was that if we put our time and energy into confronting racism and heterosexism, it would dilute our efforts to confront sexism. And since there was already such powerful resistance to acknowledging men's violence against women, let alone to mobilize efforts to stop it, we couldn't risk the possibility that we might compromise our main mission.

We couldn't see for a long time that by drawing the connections among oppressions and illumination how they both intersected and strengthen each other, we also would be strengthening the case to end violence against women. When we did make that connection, we established still another of our Core Principles, **"Intersectionality Matters."**

Meanwhile, the dynamics in the staff accountability groups themselves were intriguing. Unlike the classroom check-in, our staff and interns were checking in in the presence of men and, in some cases, women with position power. For example, staff and interns would be checking in with abusive behaviors in the presence of people who were either their supervisor or supervisee. I noticed that accountability group participants would frequently arrive late or without having thought much about their controlling behaviors before entering the room. And there was an element of carefulness and caution particularly in the way participants gave feedback.

But there were exceptions to this. One was with two of our young staff, Adam Horowitz and Trishala Deb, who took very seriously the principle of speaking truth to power. I noticed they both came to the groups prepared and were consistent in giving me feedback on the ways I used my white, male, heterosexual privilege. I also remember Red Crowley and Brian Nichols as fellow staff members who seemed unintimidated by position power and willing to bring that kind of crisp feedback to fellow staff members. I didn't always like it, but I knew I needed it.

For the most part we benefited from our accountability groups, but there were problems: sometimes staff would wonder whether if they told their supervisor how they experienced their misuse of power that challenge would be used against them. I think one of the benefits of confronting our co-workers was that when we found ourselves in public settings, like during one of our trainings, we learned to challenge participants on their sexism with more compassion and with less self-righteousness. It came from a place of wanting the other person to be able to hear the feedback and take in the parts that could have meaning for them.

For example, in our earlier years when we would do trainings, men on our staff would often be called upon to confront men in the room on their sexism. While our intention was to have these men benefit from a teachable moment, I think we were quite invested in being right and in proving ourselves trustworthy to the feminist women in the room. And the effects on the men were notable: sometimes we would hear that men felt "called out," "judged," and "humiliated." It was also interesting that when, during the question-and-answer period after one of Kathleen's presentations, one of us would confront a man in the room, that man and often others would try to pin Kathleen down (notably not us) during the break to persuade or pressure her to change her position regarding what she was saying about men and women's experience of men. We came to call those moments "late hits," since they resembled the way in which pro football players retaliate by hitting a player either out of bounds or after the whistle has blown.

Kathleen would ask us to run interference for her by engaging with those men and allowing them to discharge their anger with us before they directed it at women.

For some men it seemed to take very little "truth-telling" for them to feel provoked. But we had learned in our accountability groups that responding from a place of self-righteousness was not useful to them or for women. Those groups taught us the importance of connecting with men as a crucial part of confronting them. Connecting without colluding. During breaks we would pursue men who appeared to be struggling and invite them to share their challenges with us. We would listen and ask questions as part of our understanding their thoughts and feelings. When we then confronted them, it was a part of their experience of being heard and understood.

Even though our accountability groups produced mixed results, we wondered about offering them to other community partners who shared similar missions and similar challenges. Perhaps we didn't because we didn't get to the place where felt we had worked out our kinks, one of which was the ability to meaningfully address classism among ourselves and to challenge the ways in which class privilege affected our abilities to work with each other and with others. Even though we came from different socioeconomic backgrounds with different educational opportunities, we rarely talked collectively about how those differences impacted our treatment of our selves and others. We reflected a general tendency of those who benefit from class privilege to resist talking about the meaning of that privilege, among peers and or among those who are marginalized by it. We claimed concern about class disparity, but we didn't really deal with it.

Since I was among those who came from a background with more economic advantage, I always thought that I or we didn't talk about it because of my or our resistance to figuring out how to be accountable for those privileges. But wouldn't it be the same as how we would do accountability work around racism, sexism, or homophobia? You name how you used or benefited from it, how it affected others, what needs to be done around reparation and what you will do to address it in the future. I'm thinking that we (the advantaged *and* even the disadvantaged) were too embarrassed, if not ashamed, to acknowledge that kind of power differential—and too unwilling to take action to address it.

Another kink was the amount of time the accountability groups consumed, time that might otherwise be directed to working with men to create safety for women. Finally, there was the question of intersectionality. Which group would a black, gay man attend? If he was in the men's accountability group, did he just leave his black and gay identities at the door? For some, then, the individual accountability groups resulted in a kind of fracturing of identities. So, at one point we decided to have all staff, regardless of their self-identified social location, check in in the same accountability group. Even though that didn't seem to solve issues around power differentials, it was worth trying since accountability is hard to come by unless you build in to the fabric of your daily work.

CHAPTER 3

Community Accountability

If you want to end war and stuff you got to sing loud.
I've been singing this song now for twenty-five minutes.
I could sing it for another twenty-five minutes.
I'm not proud...or tired.

"Alice's Restaurant," Arlo Gutherie

One of our first priorities with Kathleen as executive director was to focus on the importance of language and the accurate labeling of men's violence against women. She was particularly concerned about the implications of labeling battering as a mental health problem. Gus and I could see that most of the men coming into our groups were functioning normally, if not successfully, in their public lives. Most men weren't punching out their boss at work or the cop on the corner, but they were making the choice to assault their partners in the home. So, along with many of the leading advocates around the country, we adopted the term "battering" to describe what men would do to control their partners. Battering meant men's use of emotional, psychological, and physical tactics to gain and maintain control in their relationships with women. The term "domestic violence," to this day, fails to identify agency, or who is doing what to whom, and for what purpose. We described battering as a criminal act committed most often by men against women. Like many states,

Georgia passed legislation in 1982 making simple battery, under the Family Violence Act, a misdemeanor offense.

It's notable that while we were moving away from a medical model, many of our early trainings were directed to mental health professionals, both private practitioners as well as those working in psychiatric settings. Our intention was to expose the ways that traditional therapeutic interventions were often dangerous for victims and ineffective with batterers. It was dangerous, for example, for therapists doing couples work to invite both members of the couple to disclose their understanding of the problem. While the goal was to encourage shared responsibility for the solution of the problem, too often it would result in setting the battered woman up to be punished later for her honesty.

Therapists would often argue that, using their clinical judgment, they could determine which couples were at risk for danger and that a "safety plan" for the couple could effectively prevent further violence. As clinicians ourselves, Gus and I could identify with the therapists' need to feel competent and in control of the process, but we were already hearing way too many stories from battered women who experienced a therapist's attempts to be neutral as the perfect vehicle for their batterer to blame her for provoking his abusive behavior. We also noticed that when conducting our trainings in hospital settings it was generally the line staff, social workers, and physicians' assistants who attended, while doctors and administrators who made policy and clinical decisions would, after introducing our workshop, leave to attend to "important matters." We were getting our first feel of the extent of the resistance to systemic change.

When men were first pursuing our group in Atlanta, those with more social privilege would sometimes ask if we would accept insurance for payment for their group fee. Until we decided to label battering as criminal activity, it seemed like a reasonable request. But then we began to see the class double standard in which men with "benefits" could apply them towards their group therapy while men without benefits would pay out of their pockets. It was becoming clear that paying out of pocket was the appropriate consequence for men who needed to take full responsibility, not only for the abuse they committed but also for the cost of learning how to stop it.

The mental health paradigm suggested that men who abused women were manifesting symptoms rooted in poor impulse control, low self-esteem, or an abusive family history. The "cure" called for a treatment that responded to the individual's psychopathology. Kathleen was seeing the "illness" as rooted in the culture of sexism and, consequently, required us to create interventions with men in our groups as part of a larger societal intervention. To focus on individual men would ultimately deter or distract us from addressing the culture that "infected" these men. She saw group treatment as not only reinforcing a basic misunderstanding of the root of the problem, but also a way for men to use the governing principles of psychology to protect and consolidate their male privilege. The treatment process, starting with the one-on-one interview and then progressing to signing a contract in which confidentiality was a key element, represented, in Kathleen's mind, tacit and explicit instructions that the group and its leaders were there primarily to meet the needs of the men. Men would exit that interview not understanding that the purpose and priority of the group work was to establish safety for the victim and their children.

Even the location of the group meetings held significance. When Gus and I were first running groups in Atlanta, our meetings took place at the original Quaker House on Fairview Avenue. That seemed right, because we were gathering in a place known for its commitment to peace and justice. When Kathleen hired us to conduct groups for court-mandated men in Cobb County, we met in a room in the Powder Springs Public Library. While there was general resistance to going anywhere for a mandated group for batterers, I remember thinking that men were more willing to enter a public library to meet this requirement than a mental health center, likely because men don't want to go where they might take on the stigma or label of being thought of as "sick," "mental," or "crazy."

Eventually, Quaker House moved and Gus and I began to hold our Atlanta groups in his private practice office. Most of our referrals came from therapists, but we had begun to receive referrals from the DeKalb County courts. For a while we thought about holding two separate groups, one for the court-mandated men, whom we thought of as having no choice but to be there, and one for "self-referred" men, whom we originally thought of as coming by choice.

It wasn't long before we realized that there was little, if any, difference in the attitude and beliefs of the court—and self-referred men. None of them believed that they should be there. All of them were there because someone was requiring it as a consequence of their abuse. The judge was saying go there or go to jail. Men's partners were saying go there or I'll leave or I won't come back. They weren't there because they thought they had a problem with their abuse; they were there because of their common problem of facing imposed consequences.

So we dropped the concept of separate groups and soon saw the benefits of mixing the men together. The court-referred men tended to be more real and open both in denying and claiming their abusive behavior. The self-referred men would often say things like, "Well, you know I don't have to be here. I wasn't arrested or anything like that." And pretty soon we met that remark by saying, "You just didn't get caught." Even when we changed the contract to read that the group would not maintain confidentiality to protect a man from experiencing the consequences of his criminal behavior, men, and particularly men with privilege, would assume that since they were in "group therapy" any disclosure they might make should be treated as confidential.

They had reason to question since, according to the principle of confidentiality under the psychologist's code of conduct, no therapist can release information about a client without the client's permission. Since men were disclosing information about their histories of abuse, which rightfully might be used to hold them accountable in a court of law, Gus and I met with Rob Remar, an Atlanta attorney, to determine whether our contract would nullify that privilege. Remar said that as long as we were holding a group in a private practice office with a practitioner's diploma on the wall, it didn't matter what our contract said. We would be held to the standards of the psychological code of ethics and required to maintain men's right to confidentiality.

And so, once again, we were staring at the implications of labeling both the problem and the response to the problem. It seemed the more we invested in the medical model, the more we compromised our work to hold men accountable and provide safety for battered women. It was time for a shift not only in our analysis but also in our practice.

This shift had to take place at several levels. For example, both within MSV and in the eyes of the community we had to deal with our identities as therapists. Gus and I were known in the Atlanta community for our clinical work, and some of our strongest allies, supporters, and board members came from the therapy community. We liked being able to lean into Gus's credentials as a licensed clinical psychologist. Dr. Kaufman could get us entry into places and onto panels because of his status as a psychologist. So when Kathleen began to push us to de-privatize and de-psychopathologize the problem and our understanding of the solution, we had to grapple with what that would mean to a community who saw our primary identities as therapists.

I know I struggled with the idea that we would invite our community partners to send men to MSV whose qualified certified clinicians will facilitate the group work—only we wouldn't be doing treatment, because it's not a mental health problem. In fact, in the contract that men signed to enroll in our group, men agreed to suspend any individual or couples therapy they were engaged in because we understood that each of those therapeutic modes could easily compromise his partner's safety.

In individual work, the therapist often focuses on the individual's history of psychological wounding. While we knew that his personal victimization would have to be addressed, we placed the immediate priority on his learning how to stop his controlling and abusive behavior. We saw it as unrealistic and ineffective for him to try to address his role as a victim and a perpetrator at the same time. And we could see how his individual therapist would unwittingly collude with his tendency to hold his partner responsible for his choice to abuse.

In couples work, where the therapist invites the couple to explore the ways that they share responsibility for the problem (in this case, his abuse), it put her at risk and reinforced his belief that she provokes him. So for a man to meet our contractual requirements, he would have to have an agreement with his therapist that he would suspend that work until completing the six-month MSV program. Many therapists struggled with the idea that they couldn't work with him conjointly or simultaneously. Understandably, they didn't like losing him and his client fees. And, understandably, it was hard for them to see, or for that matter accept, how we actually saw *her* as the primary beneficiary of his work with MSV. We also explained that his focusing on taking responsibility for his feelings and his actions while listening to and respecting her reality would not only be the skills that could lead to greater safety for her, but also be skills that would prepare him to be a much better candidate for individual and couples therapy. So our early trainings with therapists were often in the service of explaining our rationale for the work we were doing as well as how they, as therapists, could safely and effectively make a referral to us.

In this context, Kathleen wanted us to do something that addressed the misconceptions around the client-therapist relationship. It was really bugging her that the guy, his therapist, and, in fact, the whole community was having difficulty seeing that we were there doing what we were doing primarily for her safety. Of course, he could benefit enormously from transforming his life from one in which he was committed to dominance by any means to one in which was negotiating and sharing responsibilities. But the purpose of our work was to increase her possibilities for experiencing safety and justice.

We realized we had to do something structural, something dramatic, about our initial interaction with men to make more transparent the essential purpose of our work. Kathleen urged us to come up with a model that would say to the men referred to us, as well as to the community as a whole, that his "problem" was not a matter to be addressed in the context of a client-therapist relationship, but rather that his abuse was a violation not only of her but an offense against the acceptable norms of his community.

In response to Kathleen's request, we designed and implemented a public "orientation" as the first face-to-face contact we would have with men. In a public group gathering, we instructed men on what would be required for them to enter and complete our 24-week class for men who batter women. We spelled out the conditions of the contract, including the tuition required to pay for the course. By framing the work in educational terms, we were directly refuting the notion that mental health issues were at the root of men's battering and that men could relearn how to be strong and powerful without being overpowering and dangerous.

Orientation is also where men directly experience the importance we place on keeping agreements: men keeping agreements with other men and men keeping agreements with women, especially their partners. When promoting the orientation, we clearly communicate that in order to attend, men have to arrive between 6:30 and 7 p.m. with their $20 fee in hand. A late arrival or no fee will result in their having to come back two weeks later for the next orientation. In fact, just before locking our front door we post a sign indicating that orientation has begun, and that if they want to pursue our program they can return *on time* in two weeks.

One night when I was facilitating the orientation, I was 15 minutes into my rap when there was a loud pounding on our front door, located at the bottom of the stairs on the first floor. I advised the 18 men in the room that there was a man who had arrived late who was having difficulty accepting the consequences of his late arrival. I also requested that they join me in ignoring his efforts to get me to respond to him. His persistent pounding made him hard to ignore, but eventually he stopped and we continued on without distraction. About five minutes later, there was a huge crash just outside the door of the orientation. I realized I couldn't ignore that and asked the men to "hold on" a while I investigated the source of the noise.

When I stepped into the hallway, I encountered a rather large man who appeared dazed as he floundered around on the floor. Turns out, this was the man, whom I'll refer to as Carl, who had been pounding on our front door. When he wasn't admitted, he climbed up the side of our building, wedged open a second story hallway window, climbed through, and fell eight feet to the floor. Having lost his balance, he landed hard and awkwardly just outside the door of our orientation.

When I asked Carl what he was doing, he explained that he had scaled the building to gain entry because he couldn't go home to face his wife without attending the meeting. As I was helping him to his feet, he wanted me to know that his climbing through the window was his way of saying how motivated he is to get into our program. As I walked him back down the stairs and back out the door, he first asked me if I would call his wife to tell her how hard he tried to make the meeting.

When I told him I wouldn't be doing that, he asked me what he should tell her. I suggested that he tell her the truth: that he arrived late and when he found the door locked he was willing to break in to the second floor of the building, breaking the law in the process of trying to get his way—and that he had then justified his actions by blaming her anticipated response to his failure to make the meeting. I advised him that if he really wanted to pursue the program he'd return in two weeks on time and with his $20 fee. He did return in two weeks, on time and with his fees.

He subsequently entered the program, not missing a single class in six months and in complete compliance with all of our program requirements. I would often refer to Carl when talking to community partners about men who enter our program, particularly to partners who wonder if these are men with men mental disorders who simply can't control themselves. I explained the Carl wasn't "out of control" when he chose to climb up the side of our building. He thought of himself, like many men do, as an exceptional man with exceptional needs, for whom the rules simply don't apply. And when clear limits, boundaries and expectations were set, he was able to consistently demonstrate complete control of his behavior. This in the context of the message that says that men will demonstrate self-control and stop battering women when the community sends a clear message that their criminal behavior won't be tolerated, and that meaningful consequences will be imposed when those boundaries are violated.

One other thing about the night Carl attended orientation: as mentioned, if men don't have the $20, they are told to return with their fees at the next orientation in two weeks. Sometimes when a man appears desperate to attend the meeting we will give him the option of asking other men in the room if they will lend, or outright give, him the money for the orientation. I can't remember when we started offering that as an option, but the interesting thing is that on almost every occasion, as was true the night Carl arrived late, when a man asks other men for help, they produce the money for him. Mind you, when these men first arrive they are feeling angry and convinced that they don't belong there. Nonetheless, they would pull dollars out of their pockets until the man met his obligation. While I came to believe in the importance of expecting more of men, I also came to understand that I shouldn't underestimate the capabilities of men. Perhaps two sides of the same coin.

Changing Community Standards

Increasingly, we saw our interventions with men as effective ways to impact systems, and ultimately that strategy became the basis for the formation of our core principle, **"Community Accountability Is Key to Ending Violence Against Women."**

While we understood that the criminal-legal system was key to victim safety and batterer accountability, we were hearing battered women talk more and more about its limitations. For example, arrest and jail might result in his loss of employment, producing economic and safety challenges for her. For accountability to work for her, we needed to grow the number of community partners and institutions that would join us in sending a clear message that violence against women is unacceptable and that when a man abused a woman in her community he would experience swift and meaningful consequences—from that community.

As our notoriety grew in the early 80s, it wasn't only the psychotherapy community that pursued us: we were also invited to do a "domestic violence" workshop at Fort Benning, Georgia, one of the largest Army installations in the country. But Gus and I had mixed feelings about whether or not we should do it. On the one hand, given our commitment to promoting safety and accountability, why wouldn't we do that for women on military bases? On the other hand, would we be allowing ourselves to be part of ensuring a more effective and efficient war machine? And would we be used as a relatively minor consequence for offenders who might otherwise experience criminal or more serious charges?

Academic Community

It seemed like a recurring challenge for us as we eventually faced this same dilemma in an academic context. For example, in the late 80s Emory University contacted MSV to do a workshop for a fraternity that had designed and sold T-shirts for a charity in which the inscription read, "Put your hole on our pole," with an image of a woman sitting on a pole. As a consequence of their alleged sexual harassment of women, the men in this fraternity were required to spend two sessions with Gus and me, ostensibly to learn about the effects of men's objectification of women. Given the prevailing predatory climate on most campuses (a 1995 campus study found that one out of three college men reported that they would rape a woman if they knew they wouldn't get caught), I was sure that these men were wondering what we were doing there and why the school was making such a big deal out of nothing, especially since they were just playfully using a suggestive image of a woman for a good cause. Gus and I were questioning the efficacy of our work as well and eventually concluded that if we were to make any kind of real difference with young men at Emory we would need the backing of the Emory administration. So sometime in midwinter, we sent them a proposal in which we outlined an administrative training for the deans and the Interfraternity Council leadership regarding their roles and responsibilities in creating policies and procedures that would promote a safer climate for women on the Emory campus. Midway through the spring quarter, we got a response back that since the school was gearing up for final exams we would have difficulty getting full faculty administration participation, recommending that we postpone until the fall. By the fall, priorities had shifted and we couldn't get a meeting with the administration or faculty.

Emory was probably no better or worse than other campuses in addressing woman abuse on campus and, in fact, over the years they have brought important initiatives. Currently, Emory's James Weldon Johnson Institute fosters scholarship, teaching and public dialogue that focuses on the connection between the racism and other forms of oppression and Men Stopping Violence partners with this institute to focus specifically on the connections between racism, sexism and homophobia. But back then we could see how we were initially brought in for cosmetic purposes to discipline the frat boys with a kind of slap on the hand, with little intention to form an institutional response to the problem and, therefore, little commitment to effect the lives of women on campus.

Military Community

When we were brought to Fort Benning, we thought it might be worthwhile, because, in addition to the social service (family advocacy) staff on the post, we would be addressing commanding officers, so there was the possibility that we could reach policymakers regarding accountability for offenders.

Ours wasn't a particularly polished performance, but we found out that we were capable of working in a military setting. As men who had not participated in the military, I was wondering whether our credentials would be questioned. But they never asked and we never told. And, frankly, from the moment I walked onto that military post I felt the familiarity that comes from having gone through "basic training" described earlier in the section entitled, "we are the work."

In my version of basic training, it was coaches, P.E. teachers, and school assistant principals who spelled out performance expectations and the consequences for not meeting them. On the post, the drill instructors delivered these messages as well as the consequences for not adhering to them. So, many of the messages I got from coaches, P.E. teachers, and school assistant principals are the same messages young recruits receive from their drill instructors.

Having conducted the training at Fort Benning, Gus and I were eventually contacted to facilitate a batterers' group at Fort McPherson in Atlanta. Hierarchy or chain of command was absolutely key to how things work on a military installation, and that was true at "Fort Mac." One way that played out was that the batterers' group on base consisted entirely of enlisted men with no officers, because officers were not to mix or fraternize with men of lower rank. Of course, officers did abuse their wives but they were referred to one of our civilian groups located off-post in Atlanta. Assigning men to separate groups based on their rank sent a not-so-subtle message to officers and enlisted men, i.e., just as an officer shouldn't compromise his privileged status by disclosing his fallacies in the presence of subordinates, a man of any rank, enlisted or otherwise, should not compromise his role as head of household by acknowledging his abusive behavior to his subordinate wife.

But the chain of command also had its benefits: for example, if the officer at the top ordered or expected something, then it happened without question and with expedience. That meant that if the commanding officer on the post took intimate partner violence seriously then there would be swift response and meaningful consequences for offenders. For instance, the policy and protocol might mandate that in domestic violence incidents, military police would be dispatched and offenders would be removed from the home and confined to barracks until the family advocacy team determined that it was safe to return. These men were often referred to our group on-post, and their supervising officers monitored their attendance and participation. I can specifically recall an officer who was stationed in Germany and on a fast track for a leadership role in a combat zone. His C.O. referred him to our off-base Thursday group for 24 weeks as a condition of his regaining eligibility for combat. That officer was flown in weekly from Germany and rarely missed a session or arrived late. Upon satisfactory completion of the requirements of the group, he was deployed for combat duty. We weren't sure what that meant for his partner.

Conversely, when the commanding officer didn't take it seriously, the response to an incident was often slow and inconsistent. Compounding the consistency issue was the fact that even when you might have a C.O. who prioritized safety for victims and accountability for offenders, that C.O. could be suddenly promoted or transferred to another post, leaving his last assigned post up for grabs as far as domestic violence policy was concerned.

Regardless of the commanding officer's position on domestic violence, it was often very complicated for victims. They knew that reporting an incident of violence to the authorities could jeopardize their partner's career and compromise the mission of the military.

I'm reminded of the dilemma for Pamela Cox, wife of the iconic Atlanta Braves manager Bobby Cox. In 1995, Pamela called 911 to report that Bobby was abusing her. When she subsequently appeared before the media and the judge, she decided to drop the charges, indicating that it had not been that serious. In many of our minds, we were imagining the enormous pressure being brought on her by the entire Braves organization to give primary consideration to the importance of Bobby's reputation and the Braves' run for the pennant. What I also remember about that outcome was the domestic violence advocates in the court room reporting that Bobby was spending most of his time signing autographs as he and Pamela waited to go before the judge.

Sometimes we use military metaphors to describe victim's experiences: for example, we might say, "She is being held hostage in her own home by her batterer." This metaphor took on a special meaning during one of the trainings we conducted for the Marines on their Parris Island base in South Carolina. At one point, when we were having a discussion about what constituted safety for victims on the base, we decided to break the large group into two small groups according to their assigned responsibilities. It turned out that the military participants were all men and the advocacy staff was all women. Gus and I met with the men. Kathleen, before meeting with the women advocates, asked them where they would feel most comfortable to meet. After some hesitation, they acknowledged that the place where they would feel safest and most comfortable, the place where they could speak most honestly about the needs of victims as well as their own, was in the women's restroom.

After brainstorming in the small groups we came back together to share our findings, but it wasn't until our lunch break that Gus and I learned that the women had chosen the restroom as the most secure location to speak openly about what constituted safety for victims on that base. It was another jolting dose of women's reality, and it shed a whole other light on the work we needed to be doing with the men. It illuminated the conundrum of how to talk to those men about the women's fears without putting those women at greater risk.

It was also complicated for the military men who were referred to our batterers' group. I can remember a man in our Fort Mac group expressing confusion and frustration about how, as a member of Special Forces—by his own account, "one of the most efficient trained killers on earth"—he supposed to transform himself into a peaceful and loving parent and husband when he re-entered his home. He was, no pun intended, deadly serious about this request for help. One of the contractual agreements for enlisting in the men's group was that all participants had to place their weapons in locked storage before returning home. Gus and I also suggested that men change out of their military uniforms and into civilian clothing before returning home as a way to ritualize the changing of their roles as soldiers to family members. But it was a true challenge to address the mindset of men who were prepared to take instant and deadly action when faced with any kind of perceived threat. We maintained that even with their training, they had a choice, split-second or otherwise, as to how they would respond, whether on the battlefield or in the bedroom. It was the same message we would convey to men in all of our classes, whether they were military or not, since men would often maintain that things were happening so fast, they had no choice in the matter.

One of the most distressing incidents we ever experienced took place when a man in our group on post revealed to the group that he was so angry and jealous of his wife that he was considering killing her. She had recently moved out of their home and taken out a restraining order. Before leaving the group, Gus and me, and other men in the group, worked with him on what he could do to make sure he caused no harm to his family or himself. Immediately following the group, we reported his threat to the family advocacy team, recommending that he either be hospitalized or confined to barracks. We were clear that this was a serious threat.

Unfortunately, he was not detained. Within the three days, he had gone to his wife's place of work, shot and killed her and then himself, leaving their 8-year-old daughter without a mother or a father.

This tragic homicide-suicide was devastating for everyone who was involved with this family, including the child and her surviving family, her co-workers, the family advocacy team, and for the entire Men Stopping Violence community. We grieved for months trying to think of what we could have done to prevent it. We had to come to terms with the truth that every time we intervene with a family that's dealing with domestic violence, there is the real possibility that the victim(s) may end up being seriously injured or killed—no matter what we do. And it hastened our efforts to pay more attention to lethality assessment. Following her death, the victim's parents sued the U.S. Army for wrongful death, with the hope of recovering enough money to pay for their granddaughter's education. The legal process included deposing Gus to determine whether we had done our due diligence in informing military authorities of our extreme concern. The U.S. attorneys did their best to discourage us from testifying, at one time commenting that we would surely lose our contract with the military, and at another questioning whether we were prepared to defend allegations that one of us was gay. It wasn't long before Gus and I were relieved of our duties as group facilitators, and after the court ruled that the case could be continued on the basis of the mother's wrongful death, the United States government agreed to a significant monetary settlement in favor of her family. Twenty years later, we learned from Mark Dehler, the attorney who so skillfully represented the victim's family, the granddaughter had graduated from a distinguished university with a doctoral degree.

I've never regretted that we facilitated the group at Fort Mac. We came to appreciate the incredible courage of the military wives, the tremendous work of several of the advocates on that base, and the willingness of some of the key military officers to hold men accountable. In the final analysis, I couldn't say that the military was any better or worse than any of the other major institutions we worked with over the years when it came to holding men accountable. I always believed that one of their greatest institutional predicaments lay in the fact that the man who was usually at the top of the hierarchical pyramid, had, in his youth, received the same "basic training" as the rest of us. So, whether he was the college dean or the president, a commanding officer or a staff sergeant, a bishop or a preacher, his own sexist attitudes and beliefs would have enormous influence over the way he responded to the problem of violence against women.

Faith Community

And that brings us to our experience with faith-based communities. As alluded to earlier, our connections with Pat Merchant and Marie Fortune motivated us to find ways to partner with faith communities to mobilize their leadership to deal with violence against women. We knew that they could reach and influence as many, if not far more, men than any of the institutional leaders with which we might work. The temple, the church, and the mosque are the places men and women visit to explore their personal beliefs regarding ethics, morality, relationships, survival, success, oppression, and liberation.

In 1990, Rev. Marie Fortune, executive director of the national center for the Prevention of Sexual and Domestic Violence (now known as FaithTrust, www.faithtrustinstutute.org), invited us to join her in partnering with faith leaders from the National Council of Churches (NCC) to provide an interdenominational training for men and women clergy regarding their roles and responsibilities in ending violence against women in their faith communities.

Having learned from our work with men in general and from the principles underlying "we are the work," we knew that male clergy would have to address their own sexism if they were to confront it in their congregations. So, Kathleen and Marie conceived of a dynamic training model, which we would employ in our trainings for years to come. The core of the training was built on a series of structured experiential exercises designed to facilitate men's understanding of women's experience of the full range of men's violence against women. We wanted to discourage men from intellectualizing and objectifying women's experience of men's violence and encourage their feeling and personalizing that experience.

We started the training by placing men and women in same sex groups to share their earliest memories of violence against women: who committed what violence, what was said and done in response to that violence, and what they learned from that response. We then shifted to a larger group conversation about what and how those experiences shaped their attitudes towards victims and perpetrators with a significant amount of time addressing how much the participants learned to blame the victim.

The core of the training was a structured sequence of "fishbowls": in the first fishbowl, the female clergy sat in circle facing each other, responding to a series of questions composed by Marie and Kathleen. The questions were designed to illuminate how these women experienced their male colleagues treating women in their congregations: women who were congregants, staff, peers, and themselves. Meanwhile, male clergy were seated just outside the women in a concentric circle and their task was to listen without commenting on or interrupting the process and to pay attention to when they were having strong feelings about what was being shared.

After an hour of the women sharing their process, and a brief break, the male clergy were invited to reconvene in the inner circle while the women sat in the surrounding circle with the instruction to listen and to pay attention to their feelings. The male clergy were instructed first to share what they learned from the women about the women, and then what they learned about themselves. They were specifically instructed not to critique the women's observations. For some men this was a revelatory and transforming experience. Particularly, as they had not had the experience of women peers and/or subordinates commenting on how they were experienced as men. For some men it was agonizing to sit and listen to difficult truths without being able to immediately respond, critique, or defend. But it clearly altered the nature of the relationships in the room, some for the better, and some maybe not.

Later in the training, we asked the male clergy to put themselves on our Controlling Behaviors Checklist (an inventory that identifies men's pattern of abuse against women) as a way for them to prepare to hold men in their congregations accountable. We had done a version of this fishbowl/checklist experience previously with therapists and we noticed a similarity in the difficulty they experienced in claiming their use of negative behaviors, likely because both male therapists and clergy aren't accustomed to inviting and then getting feedback on how women experience them. They were, I think, more accustomed to inviting others to take stock or accountability for their lives than for doing so with their own.

Two clergymen, one white and one a man of color, were particularly resistant to listening to women's experience of them, both in the training, and, apparently, in their congregations back home. Marie and Kathleen asked Sulaiman Nuriddin, another MSV facilitator about whom we'll learn more later, and me to team up and meet with each of these men individually to assist them in dealing with their denial and minimization. It seemed that for each of these men it was more important for them to establish themselves as more unlike us than like us . . . no matter what we said to connect with them or to confront them.

Sulai and I felt like we blew it. The women said that it was helpful to know that it wasn't just women who couldn't get through to them, that they felt freer to put their energy elsewhere and could now focus more on men with more potential to be allies. In that way, it seemed useful.

There were also men for whom, it seemed, the proverbial light bulb went on. Sure, they were struggling with some of the pain and guilt that comes with owning up to their controlling behaviors, but they seemed more energized than paralyzed by it. And they wanted to go deeper with it. They wanted to bring it to a broader constituency of their denomination.

The Mennonite men in the room, for example, requested a three-day training for men and women clergy to work on the same issues we had worked on with reps from the NCC training. Several months before the Mennonite training, Kathleen contacted the women clergy who would participate in the training to get their input on the structure of the training. During the course of her communications with those women, four of them disclosed that, as young women, John Howard Yoder, a premier Mennonite theologian who had been a primary mentor in their lives, had sexually abused them. Kathleen realized that whatever else the training accomplished, we would need to create a safe space for the women to participate and, if they so chose, to reveal their victimization to their fellow Mennonite clergymen.

Now, I noticed that when I first wrote this paragraph I experienced some hesitation in using Yoder's name. Was I singling him out? Defaming him? He's not that different from other men I've described and not named in this book. On the other hand, I can recall the powerful sentiments of Barbara Hart, who long ago challenged women and men in our movement to refrain from protecting perpetrators by not naming them, noting the isolating effect it has on survivors, who often feel pressured to protect their abusers from public scrutiny. So, here I am intentionally naming John Yoder—not because he's special, but because he's not.

Borrowing from the earlier training we had done with the NCC, we first asked the whole group to explore their earliest memories of violence against a woman. Later in the training, when we came to the women's fishbowl exercise, the women with whom Kathleen had been communicating shared their victimization by the Mennonite theologian. It was an act of extraordinary courage in that, even though we had prepared the men by putting them through a series of intense listening exercises, we didn't know if they would believe the women. We didn't know whether, in the face of the men's love and loyalty for this distinguished Mennonite minister, they would choose to stand in solidarity with their sisters. As it happened, the women's telling of their individual stories was so heart-wrenching and courageous the men in the room were overwhelmed with grief and compassion for the women. And they were, as I remember it, also in a spiritual crisis. I think they were clear about wanting to provide an initial authentic and caring response to the women, but they were clearly confounded by what to do with their thoughts and feelings about a man who had not only deeply betrayed these women, but an entire denominational community.

The women waited to hear from the men and particularly whether their response would include an intention to hold their abuser accountable. As in the previous interdenominational training, we asked the Mennonite men to claim their patterns of abuse in relationships with women. Led by the Mennonite men who had participated in the earlier training, the men seemed to understand the importance of taking responsibility for their behavior as a necessary step towards holding men accountable; in light of the women's disclosures, this seemed particularly relevant if they were to hold their mentor accountable. Once the men committed to taking action, the women requested that they meet and come up with an accountability plan that would result in compassionately confronting him while not putting the women in further danger.

In actuality we didn't learn the outcome of their accountability process until relatively recently when I went on line and found a September 29, 1992, newspaper report from the *Elkhart (Indiana) Truth* titled "John Howard Yoder's Sexual Misconduct," in which news reporter Tom Price wrote:

> The ministerial credentials of John Howard Yoder, regarded as one of this century's leading theologians and ethicists were suspended Saturday by a regional Mennonite Church Commission over allegations of his sexual misconduct.
>
> Yoder, professor of Christian ethics at the University of Notre Dame and a former professor at that Associated Mennonite Biblical Seminary here, has cooperated with an 11-month investigation by two Mennonite Church panels into allegations presented in testimony by eight women. "The charges brought by the women are accurate and John has violated sexual boundaries," according to a task force at Prairie Street Mennonite Church of which Yoder is a member. "John has acknowledged the truth of the charges and has expressed deep regret for the hurt his actions have caused the women. The women, who are on positions of national church leadership, said the allegations

included improper hugging, use of sexual innuendo, or overt sexual language, sexual harassment, kissing or attempts to kiss women, nudity and violent sexual behavior. Sexual intercourse was not among the allegations."

This marks the third investigation into the allegations of Yoder's misconduct since rumors first came to the attention of Mennonite officials in the 1970s, leading some to call for his resignation from the seminary. According to a source close to the investigation, Goshen Biblical Seminary examined similar allegations but dropped the matter in 1984 when Yoder ended his seminary employment. Since then he has taught Christian ethics at the University of Notre Dame, where he has been an adjunct faculty member since 1977.

While this article notes that Yoder's ministerial credentials were suspended in 1992, when asked about the implications of Yoder's sexual misconduct, Lawrence S. Cunningham, then chairman of Notre Dame's theology department, responded, "I am distressed to hear about the action of the Mennonite Church. But it is my understanding that these events occurred before professor Yoder came to Notre Dame. It is not clear to me that his standing in this university is affected by the actions of his church. That is not to say that the university condones that kind of behavior."

Wow. So isn't this a case of a classic slap on the wrist? It looks like the panel of Mennonite men and women were able to get him to claim responsibility and regret for his abuse, but in terms of consequences,

Yoder reportedly didn't care anywhere near as much about his preaching privileges as his teaching privileges. And while there may have been a mixed response from the Mennonite community of higher education regarding their openness to his continuing to teach, it looks like Notre Dame issued a full pass. As for restitution, only the accounts of the survivors could determine whether they felt meaningfully vindicated. My attempts to reach them have not been successful.

Two other notes on this: first, I learned from one of the Mennonite men who attended our Colorado Mennonite MSV Conference that he and two other men who attended that conference have been in the same ongoing men's support/accountability group they formed at the conclusion of that gathering 22 years ago. Second, the women who came forward with the charges against Yoder insisted that their names remain anonymous throughout the process. While some members of the Mennonite community expressed concern that it was unfair to Yoder to protect the women's anonymity, denying Yoder the opportunity to defend himself, it reminded me of the thinking and the strategy of the women advocates on the Marine Base at Parris Island, who knew that in the context of that male centered institution, the extent of their safety could be measured in terms of the dimensions of the women's bathroom.

Challenged Communities

Community trainings were often the vehicle through which we challenged communities to find ways to end violence against women. But the general public persisted in wanting to know if our batterers program was "successful." No matter what we said about the importance of community accountability and about the pitfalls of focusing on evaluating individual programs and the men participating in them, people would ask, "But does your program stop men from battering women?"

In 1995, the U.S. Centers for Disease Control and Prevention (CDC) awarded MSV a five-year demonstration grant to measure the effectiveness of the batterers' program in influencing community norms that could stop men's violence against women. Kathleen conceived of this study to shift the focus from measuring the efficacy of individual batterers programs to measuring the community's attitudes and responses to men's abuse of women. In her words:

> "The design of our evaluation project is an effort to shift the discourse away from the question, 'What is your success rate with individual batterers?' to instead, 'How are diverse communities moving toward establishing and enforcing norms that say battering will not be tolerated here?'"[7]

The basic idea was to intervene in two suburban counties with the purpose of improving the effectiveness of the community response to domestic violence, particularly the response of the criminal-legal system. MSV staff teamed with researchers from Georgia State and Emory universities, the University of Alabama, and UCLA. In accordance with the proposal, Red Crowley and Brian Nichols worked under the supervision of Kathleen as the principal investigator to provide trainings and public awareness campaigns for faith communities, the business community, print and broadcast media, mental health communities, educational institutions, and the criminal-legal system.

In the second year of the project, Kathleen went on a writing sabbatical with Red continuing as the project director. Shortly after her return, and in a totally unexpected and devastating development, Kathleen was diagnosed with lung cancer. She died within six months of her diagnosis and in the midst of that overwhelming loss the project team had to regroup and continue on. It was a spectacular display of tenacity, courage and resourcefulness.

Meanwhile, our staff, her family and friends, and our community partners and supporters locally and nationally, were stunned and heartbroken by our loss. The transition and adjustments that our staff experienced will be covered in more detail in the section entitled **"Race Matters."** But, for the CDC project, Kathleen's death created a huge void that was ultimately addressed when Libby Cates Robinson, a former MSV board member and an active Atlanta feminist, stepped in and took over as the principal investigator.

Red Crowley describes how, when presenting at CDC seminars, he and Kathleen would begin by saying that "batterers' programs don't work" as a provocative way to introduce the idea that batterers' programs are only as effective as the norm-setting institutions around them at stopping men's battering. Ultimately, far more energy went into educating the CDC than was originally anticipated. So while the findings of the project confirmed that the chief norm-setters in a community, such as the chief superior court judge, determine whether a community response is effective, it was the education of the CDC that probably had the most meaningful and unintended benefits.

Though the project produced several crucial findings, there was one in particular that spoke to the challenges inherent in creating and then measuring community accountability: even though the

CDC selection committee picked our proposal because of its unique perspective on measuring effective community-based ways to stop domestic violence, as soon as we began meeting with the CDC implementation team, they insisted on asking us when and how we would measure recidivism rates for the batterers going through our program. So, even after it was explicitly stated in our proposal that we would *not* be focusing on the individual outcomes of batterers, their repeated inquiries about individual batterers spoke to their inability or unwillingness to measure community rather than individual change.

That resistance mirrored in many ways the widespread resistance we experience to this day to focus on the role of the entire community, and particularly men in the community, to stop violence against women. But as we struggled with whether to direct our energies towards fixing "flawed" men or finding the men who could stop them, it seemed we had to figure out how to do both.

CHAPTER 4

Organizing Men

She's not asking what you're gonna tell your daughter.
She's asking what you're going to teach your son.

From the poem, "Blue Blanket," by Andrea Gibson

Because of experiences like the one we had with the CDC, we needed to clarify our reasons for the importance of mobilizing men in general to join us in our work. We needed to formulate our case in the form of a Core Principle and then, with consistency, put it into practice. That principle became "Organizing men to end violence against women takes precedence over intervening with batterers."

The practice took on many iterations, and some of our best practice emerged out of totally unplanned strategies.

Such was the case when we were dealing with a man (whom I will refer to here as Al), who was nearing the end of his work in our Monday night class for batterers. Two weeks prior to his completing the course, he announced to his partner (whom we will refer to as Sue) that he was ready to start a batterers' class for the men in their church. Sue forewarned me of his plans when she called to say that she wondered what he was thinking since a majority of their fellow parishioners, including many of the men, were incensed by his brutalization of her and their children. As Al was preparing for his final peer and self-evaluation, I called on him to acknowledge that I had heard that he was planning to start up a batterers' group for men in his congregation. He confirmed my report and wanted me to know that it was his transformative experience in the MSV program that inspired him to want to help other men. I acknowledged his positive intentions and said that the best way to orient men from his church to the work he was doing was to bring at least two of them to witness his final review. I wouldn't have been surprised if he had shown up without any men, but three men came with him for his final review. And when it came time for the men in Al's class to give him feedback on the work he had done over the 24-week period, we decided to invite the three men from Al's church to participate in that process.

When they did, it was telling.

When asked how they experienced Al, both in the class and in previous experiences of him out in the community, they had a lot to say. They told him how horrified they were by his abuse of Sue and by the devastating effects it had on her and their children. They claimed feelings of confusion, distrust, and anger. They were confused by his forthright claiming of his abuse, which so contrasted with his denial, minimizing and blaming when they were with him prior to the class. They felt distrust because they doubted his sincerity and they were angered by his audacity to think that men would look to him for help. They referred to experiences of him that we didn't know of and they confronted him in ways that we couldn't because they were a part of his lived everyday life.

Al was shaken by the depth of their honesty and concern for Sue and their children, and for him. The rest of us in the room were blown away by their willingness to bring truths that were so compelling and so beyond our abilities to know. They agreed that upon his completion of the class they would meet with him periodically to monitor his progress and to hold him accountable. And when, at the end of the class, we asked the men from the church to share what they had learned, they noted that they were not only impressed by class participants' willingness to take responsibility for their abuse and to respectfully challenge each other, they became aware of how they themselves were guilty of using some of those same behaviors with their partners, never having thought of them as being abusive or controlling.

What I learned—again—was that if you expect more of men, in this case Al and the men from his church, they will do more. And this experience further motivated us to explore ways in which we could use men from our batterers' program to mobilize men from their communities.

We had already created our Community Restoration Program (CRP) for men who had completed our 24-week program, who wanted to assist us in our work and who had demonstrated an understanding of the need to restore to their community what they destroyed when they abused their partners. For years those men had been assisting us at our orientation for classroom candidates by describing their worst incident of violence against a woman, and, in so doing, publicly modeling accountability for their violence.

Over time, we needed and they wanted to do more to educate men in general (not just batterers) regarding their roles and responsibilities in ending violence against women.

In 2005, CRP was provided a great opportunity when the U.S. Department of Justice's Office on Violence Against Women (OVW) requested organizations throughout the country to support reauthorization of funding for the Violence Against Women Act

(VAWA). These funds had provided essential services for battered women nationwide since 1994. But there was a serious threat to the funding process in 2005 when right-wing men's organizations were frantically lobbying against VAWA reauthorization, claiming that OVW women discriminated against men by only providing funding for services for women. Their contention was that women are as violent as men in intimate partner relationships and, therefore, men should, under federal regulations, be entitled to an equitable share of the funding. These men may have seemed far-fetched, but they were serious and very well organized. They were consistently showing up to lobby key U.S. legislators and it became clear that pro-feminist men needed to step up our efforts to support VAWA.

In Georgia that meant reaching out to key Senate and House members to educate them regarding the importance of reinstating VAWA. CRP men organized a statewide campaign under the name of Men Supporting VAWA, first targeting Sen. Johnny Isaakson with the hope of enlisting his support to co-sign on the bill. When setting up the meeting, CRP was given 15 minutes with the senator to make the case. Soon after they were in the room, the senator asked why, as men, they were there lobbying for funding for services for women. One by one they disclosed that they had battered their partners, explaining how batterers, including themselves, can more easily manipulate and control their partners when there are inadequate support services for battered women. They were making the case that it is in their interest as men that their loved ones live in safe and violence-free relationships. Forty-five minutes into the meeting Sen. Isaakson's administrative aide stepped in to say it was time to wrap it up. By then the senator had gained some important information and some newfound respect for men who were modeling accountability in the service of progressive social legislation. The senator did not sign on as a cosponsor of the bill, but he did, in the end, vote for reauthorization.

Each year, prior to the Georgia legislative session, battered women's legislative advocates would attend a CRP meeting to educate men regarding bills that would be introduced that would either aid or be injurious to battered women. As a result, CRP men were prepared to join women advocates at the state capitol in the lobbying process. They had to know the bill and be able to effectively argue for or against it in what is sometimes referred to as an elevator speech. That is, in making the case they had to be brief and to the point, as in capable of delivering the message in the time that it would take an elevator to go from the bottom to the top floor. Clearly, they wouldn't have time to self-identify as batterers and, unlike the experience with Sen. Isaakson where they did have time to establish a relationship, it most likely would have undermined their "credentials" as lobbyists.

For example, in 2007, CRP joined advocates testifying at state legislative hearings to oppose the presumption of joint custody in child custody cases. They argued that because many cases of contested divorces involve violence against women and children, joint custody could give perpetrators unsafe access to victims. Subsequent to the hearings, the language in the legislation was adjusted to address these concerns. CRP men weren't saying anything unique or different from the women advocates, but it did seem to make a difference that men were saying it.

Another CRP opportunity occurred when a Georgia criminal justice study found that victims and their perpetrators are more inclined to turn to their faith communities for help than to shelters or the criminal legal system. In 2010, a Georgia Commission on Family

Violence Fatality Review report confirmed that faith communities play a significant role in preventing domestic violence. Since there were men from CRP who had leaned into their spiritual beliefs and practices to change their abusive behaviors, they were motivated to reach out to faith communities, particularly faith-based men's groups, to grow the number of men who could speak up to prevent domestic violence. They created a 90-minute interactive workshop (MAPP or Men's Awareness Program Presentation), inviting men to explore men's roles and responsibilities to make their communities safer for women and children.

In each of these initiatives, CRP men found innovative ways to connect with other men who could use their influence and sometimes affluence to prevent violence against women. Upon completing the 24-week MSV Men's Education Program, they seemed to have concluded that to change their own attitudes, beliefs, and behaviors towards women was important but not enough; feeling bad about and taking responsibility for their violence was important but not enough. They understood that for them to stay on track they needed to grow the number of men around them who could share their awareness and their work. Having experienced a change in the quality of their relationships with loved ones, friends and colleagues, they saw it as in their self-interest to educate other men.

Because We Have Daughters®

Many of our supporters and allies have asked us, "Why would men want to join Men Stopping Violence in their mission when by merely being associated with us, it could make them look and or feel bad?" For example, some men might say that those who support men stopping violence are helping women but in so doing they're trashing men. Shelley Serdahley, MSV's executive director from 2003 to 2012, decided to answer that question by creating an MSV initiative called Because We Have Daughters˙ (BWHD).

Her thinking was that men want to work to end violence against women because they have daughters whom they want to be able to grow up and be fully who they want to be and be physically and emotionally safe in their relationships with boys and men. So, we designed an experiential workshop for dads and their daughters where the dads could deepen their understanding and their support for their daughters by engaging in a series of fun and intriguing games and activities. One of the things we knew going into these workshops is that most dads sincerely want to do right by their daughters, to say and do the right things when it really matters. We also know that instinctively, when dads become aware of their daughter(s) having a problem, they want to fix it. They want to do something. And often, their daughters don't necessarily need their dads or anyone to do something. First and foremost they may need their dads to listen, to understand and to empathize with their concerns before any action is taken by anyone. Having listened to young women about their needs, MSV's Because We Have Daughters˙ program created some Core Values which would be the basic take-home lessons from the workshop. Those core values include:

Understand the societal pressures women and girls face. All girls and women live with the knowledge that they could be assaulted by someone they know or even love. BWHD provides an opportunity for men to learn what it is like to live with that knowledge and how it shapes women's reality.

Listen. Listening is the most important communications skill. Actively listening to your daughter lets her know that you value what she has to say.

Be mindful of space. Men are often unaware of the amount of physical, verbal, and emotional space they occupy in relation to women and girls. BWHD activities build awareness of the need to provide space for girls to expand their identity and grow into their full potential as women.

Pause. Fathers are encouraged to pause in different situations to allow time and space for their daughters. For example, a father may pause during a conversation to hear another view or during activities to ensure that everyone is included.

Practice assertiveness instead of aggression. Understanding the distinction between assertiveness and aggression is important. Both fathers and daughters get opportunities to practice assertiveness and to challenge aggressive behaviors.

Appreciate non-traditional qualities. Fathers can encourage daughters to explore a full range of possibilities for their lives by expressing appreciation for daughters' non-traditional qualities.

Discuss difficult issues without judgment. Fathers who learn to listen actively without blaming, minimizing or judging can strengthen relationships with their daughters. This also provides space for fathers to counsel without regret.

Share decision-making equitably. The process of sharing ideas in a respectful way is as important as resolving a situation. In interactions with their daughters, fathers are used to coming up with "the answer" to a challenge or conflict, but allowing open discussion leaves space for girls to explore their own ideas with confidence.

(For more, see Appendix A.)

Because We Have Daughters' has provided workshops for men and their daughters in faith communities, in school settings, and on military installations. Workshop evaluations tell us that the father-daughter interactions have been profoundly instructive. But perhaps equally important was the time the dads met together to problem-solve about how to be most supportive to their daughters during the workshop and, subsequently, at home. During one of the fathers' "circles," when asked what he would offer in the way of support to his daughter who was just beginning to date, one of the dads opined, "First thing I'd tell her that if he so much as lays a finger on your body I'll take him to the woodshed." There was an initial response of laughter from the other men. Then, after some silence, they began to consider what his statement was conveying to her about her own abilities to make decisions and to protect herself, about her ability to assert her needs with a boy or, for that matter, with her father. Men invited him to consider that the woodshed response might be meeting his needs, but not hers; to consider practicing the Core Values as a way to support her and empower her in dating relationships. When the group meeting was finished at the end of 45 minutes, the men were clearly not finished. They were hungry to continue the conversation, sharing doubts, fears, and concerns for their daughters, and for their capacity to "show up" for them.

Some men acknowledged that they thought that when their daughters reached puberty it was their "job" to step aside and let the mom take over the parenting since she would be more "qualified" to address issues around their daughters' sexuality. Men were invited to consider that this was a time when they really needed to be present and available, not intrusive, in their daughters' lives. They were asked to consider the importance of what they could share, if they were asked, about male sexuality. They were encouraged to consider that by modeling the Core Values with their daughters, it would be a wonderful way for their daughters to learn about what they could expect in a relationship with boys and men their own age. We could also see how hungry men are to share their experiences as dads with other men. Inevitably those conversations would lead to their concerns around "manhood" and "masculinity" and the challenges they faced growing up as boys relating to girls and now as men relating meaningfully to their partners and their children.

We hadn't anticipated that gay couples would show up for these workshops to struggle with the same questions. When it came time for the dads to meet and there were two dads in the room who were there as a couple, we had to deal with men's homophobia, in this case men's fear and hatred of men loving men, and men's heterosexism, or the belief that heterosexual couples are the only acceptable, normal love affiliations. Our lack of preparation revealed our own heterosexism since it apparently didn't occur to us that same-sex parents would pursue Because We Have Daughters˚. And once again we found that our mistake opened up an opportunity for our facilitators to more directly deal with homophobia and its connection to sexism. The ways that our fears of getting close and real with each other as men inhibits us from getting important emotional support from other men while at the same time encouraging us to expect, if not demand, emotional support from women.

The opportunities for engaging with men in general seem limitless, because men, whether we acknowledge it or not, are always trying to figure out how to be men. One of the interesting and consistent responses to our Because We Have Daughters' initiative has been, "Well, this is great for daughters, but what are you doing for our sons? When all is said and done they're the ones who really need the help and if you reach them when they're young you can break the cycle." This, by the way, comes as vociferously from women as from men. I have to say that part of me has wondered whether some of that concern is rooted in some deeply held resistance to thinking of the needs of girls being as important as those of boys. We found some irony in the fact that as the dads became more sensitized to how to respond to the hopes and fears expressed by their daughters, they became much better prepared to teach and intervene with boys. Just as listening in on the battered women's hotline helped us to know why and how to respond to their male partners, listening to daughters has given dads a more comprehensive sense of why and how to talk to boys.

However, to address this concern more directly, MSV has, over the years, offered programs designed to prepare men on college campuses to mentor young men and boys at the secondary school level. Since we're Atlanta-based, that often meant preparing students at all-male Morehouse College to mentor inner-city youth, specifically young, African-American males who are at risk of dropping out because they had bought into the message that to try to succeed academically was a "white thing," if not "soft." So, the core of this program was based on creating opportunities for deconstructing "strength" and focusing on the costs and the benefits of adopting hyper masculine strategies for achieving success.

The mentors weren't trying to preach to these young men. They knew that young men tend to watch what we do more than what we say. And I know from my own experience how our son, Sam, while he heard versions of my "MSV rap" over the years, paid much more attention to how I *treated* his mom and other women than to what I *said* about that. Knowing this, mentors invited young men in one-to-one and group settings to share their beliefs about how to achieve the things that really mattered to them: jobs, relationships, possessions. The mentors would listen and respectfully challenge young men to bring a deeper level of consciousness to their choice-making process. Part of their preparation for mentoring required the mentors to examine their own socialization on matters of race and sex, so that when younger men would ask them to get real about how they figured these things out they could speak with integrity about their choice-making, including mistakes, consequences and successes.

CHAPTER 5

Race Matters: The Conundrums

Until the killing of black mothers' sons is as important as the killing of white mothers' sons, we who believe in freedom cannot rest.

"Ella's Song," Bernice Johnson Reagon,
Sweet Honey in the Rock

M en's use of force and violence is key to the discussion of masculinity. In our Men's Education Program, one of the conditions for participation is an agreement that, when disciplining children, corporal punishment is not acceptable. For many men, that has seemed workable, but for many other men, particularly men of color, that choice has been problematic if not unacceptable. Unacceptable because of the belief that if you spare the rod, you spoil the child, that the alternatives to corporal punishment are "white," "apologetic," and ineffective with children of color.

Our response has often been to ask the question, "What is the take-home lesson you're wanting for your child: to learn to fear or to learn to respect? To learn to fear the consequence and the person imposing it, or to learn respect for the limit itself and the person setting it? Can you teach respect for rules and limits without instilling fear and without sending the message that using physical force is the accepted and preferred way to solve conflicts or problems?"

Interesting questions. But if you don't acknowledge and demonstrate respect for cultural differences it won't get very real in the room. Men and women won't be willing to speak honestly from the perspective of their unique cultural lens. It was from continually running into this truth in our trainings, in community presentation, in our classes, sometimes addressing it, sometimes not, that we came to adopt the Core Principle, **"Race Matters."**

In our classes for men we routinely invite men to look at and claim the ways that they use and benefit from male privilege. In so doing, we refer to the tactics described in the Power and Control Wheel, developed by the Domestic Abuse Intervention Project in Minnesota, in which male privilege is defined as "making all the decisions, acting like the master of the castle, defining men's and women's roles, treating her like a servant."

The exercise is challenging for all men but we noticed that for men of color this assignment was particularly vexing. Often men, and African-American men in particular, would respond with a version of "What are we talking about here? Let's get real. I don't have that kind of privilege. Wish I did have some of it. You're talking about white men who have freely used those tactics not only on women, but also on me. You're certainly not talking about me and my experience with black women."

In my mind there was more than a grain of truth in what they were saying, but not all of it. And, it's complicated.

African-American men deal day-to-day with racism and its virulent forms of white privilege; it affects their own sense of agency and esteem, and it affects the way they experience and treat black women. One way I've begun to understand these conundrums is to recall, some 25 years ago, bell hooks, author and activist, responding to a question posed by one of her readers following one of her recitations at Charis Books in Atlanta. The questioner was asking bell to comment on the efficacy of couples therapy in the African-American community. The therapist part of me was immediately intrigued by the question, but I was totally unprepared for bell's response. I heard bell saying, in effect, that given the legacy of survival for African-American couples on slave plantations, given the terrible truths of what African-American women endured at the hands of their slave owners in the form of rampant rape and sexual harassment, given the felt need for African-American women to protect themselves and their husbands from knowing of these atrocities and from the deadly consequences of retaliating to them, it resulted in their withholding and suppressing the sharing of their deepest and most painful truths. Protecting black men from knowing the truth became an essential means of survival for African-American women. And, of course, this horrific humiliation was compounded by the white community's tactic of projection, fabricating myths and accusations of black men sexually assaulting white women—and then acting on those fabrications in the form of lynching.

So, having bell's explication ringing in my ears as I facilitated classes with a mixture of white and black men, how could I not know the meaning of this legacy and the layered risks involved for black men to expose the truth of their mistreatment of black women in the presence of white men? They not only risked white men using that information to reinforce and then act upon stereotypic beliefs about black men and their violence, they risked breaking the unspoken code of silence as an essential means of surviving the brutal tactics of white supremacy. The conversation going on in my head was not the first and only place this conundrum was being considered by the MSV community.

In the early 1990s, Kathleen had invited key African-American stakeholders from the MSV board and the community at large to address the specific needs of black women and the ways that MSV's mission was and wasn't meeting their needs. Soon a group of radical thinkers, writers, orators, and activists formed to sharpen our analysis and strengthen our practice in our work with the African-American community. Led by African-American women, they created their own operating model and named it the African-American Initiative (AAI). Loretta Ross, MSV board member and founder of several national social justice organizations, characterized this initiative as a think tank, more advisory in its role and more inclined to make MSV's work more relevant to the needs of black women than to create entire new programs. When Loretta wasn't setting up a national organization to monitor the Klan and other hate groups, she was heading up a national organization Sister Song, which draws the connection between reproductive and human rights. Loretta was joined in AAI by, among others, Thandabantu Iverson, activist and academician whose areas of interest include feminist theory, African-American political thought and labor studies and human rights; Quiyama Rahman, now an ordained Unitarian Universalist minister, who in the 90s was a powerful advocate for battered women all over the state of Georgia; Sandra Barnhill, MSV board member and founder and director of the groundbreaking national organization, Aid to Imprisoned Mothers (now Forever Family), whose vital mission is to promote ongoing healthy relationships between children and their incarcerated mothers and fathers.

Sandra remembers how Kathleen wisely decided that AAI would be connected to MSV, but not under its direction. It functioned in an advisory capacity and, since two of its members, Sulaiman and Ulester Douglas, were staff and three of its members served on the MSV board, there was an element of mutual accountability, both to the mission of MSV and to the vision of AAI.

The structure and the process of the meetings was more, to coin a term of those times, afrocentric and, therefore, the working relationships among the men and women reflected some of the need of African-American women to work in partnership and in collaboration with their African-American brothers. Since patriarchy requires the oppression of women in all racial and ethnic groups, including among men and women of color, African-American men weren't exempt from being held accountable to the women in the African-American Initiative. But the emphasis on partnership and collaboration was an intentional way to heal the relational wounds inflicted, during slavery and beyond, by racists and racism. And, at that time, it reflected a movement-wide difference in the way that many white women were dealing with men who had not dealt with their male privilege.

White women were facing some of the same challenges that confronted Kathleen and Lee Ann when they were supervising Gus and me. What were our true intentions? Would we ultimately work to co-opt feminist thinking and funding to further our own interests? Could we be true allies and, if so, how would we demonstrate our solidarity? And it's not that women of color weren't wondering those same things about men of color, but that they were doing so in a context where the legacy of racism had created debilitating splits in their families and communities and they were searching for ways to address gender oppression without furthering the effects of racial oppression.

Meeting monthly over a two-year period, AAI produced several compelling recommendations. Recognizing that some, if not many, African-American men would not feel as free to address their abuse of women in the presence of white men, using their own experience of oppression as an excuse for not dealing with their roles as oppressors, they proposed an all African-American class, facilitated by African-American men and offered as a choice for African-American men. (There are also many African-American men who elect to participate in mixed-race class.) For the all African-American class, the goals and objectives around safety and accountability were consistent with those of the other classes. But the content and process were altered to honor African-American cultural traditions and to create space to draw parallels between the abuse of power they experienced at the hands of the criminal-legal system and the abuse of power they used in their relationships with women.

AAI also recognized the absence of African-Americans in positions of decision-making power on the board and staff of Men Stopping Violence. Given that a substantial portion of our work in Atlanta focused on promoting safety for African-American women, it was clear that we needed African-American women and men with real position power who could shape policies and practices that affected the lives of African-American families.

Subsequent to their recommendations, African-American women and men assumed position-power responsibilities at both the board and staff levels, including Ulester Douglas as Co-executive Director and Sulaiman Nurridin as Director of Men's Education.

With these appointments came some meaningful shifts in our program priorities. In a city with a significant black population (Atlanta is 57 percent African-American), we felt that our strategic interventions had to intentionally meet the challenges and needs of that community. So, in our classes, our community education and training, in our internship, mentoring project and BWHD, we focused on providing resources and programs that promote safety and justice for African-American women and girls.

For example, with Because We Have Daughters we recruited and worked closely with faith leaders in the African-American community to establish the dad-daughter experiences. Atlanta is like many southern cities in that if it doesn't have a place of worship on every corner, you're usually not more than a few blocks from finding one of your choice. When we decided to place a special emphasis on reaching out to African-American men in communities to join us in creating safer communities, it was a no-brainer that we'd look to the church. And we quickly figured out that, as in the case with the commanding officers and campus deans, if the pastor, the imam or the rabbi were into the program, it would happen, and clearly the most notable successes took place when the pastor participated in the program as a dad.

I felt particular appreciation for Gary Taylor, an African-American preacher from Open Word Ministries, who made sure that he had a healthy showing of dads and daughters "in the room." But equally important was that he shared the same rich learning experiences with his daughter and other dads that he had recruited. He also had the kind of charisma and courage that allowed him to share with dads some of the struggles he was engaged in with his daughters.

One reason we were directing our attention to faith communities was because of our awareness of the shortcomings of the criminal-legal system. We had listened to battered women describe what it's like to navigate that system: call the police, maybe he gets arrested or maybe they both get arrested and, after a lecture from the police officer he or both spend 24 hours in jail, get bonded out and by then he's incensed and, along with other interested parties, blaming her for his losing his job or a job possibility or for not adequately protecting the kids or herself. Then she's subjected to a lecture on how the courts are now completely biased in favor of her and women, followed by threats regarding what he'll do if she calls the police again. And, if she's undocumented . . . let us pray.

Who in their right mind would subject themselves to this kind of unpredictable and treacherous outcome? You? Me? Probably not.

But advocates all over the state of Georgia, including MSV, have been working to tweak the system. So, it's not been an all or nothing question for us. We figured that if we were going to urge victims to look to alternatives to the criminal-legal system for safety and justice we'd have to step up our efforts to educate other community institutions to meet those needs, while at the same time pushing for greater performance from the legal system itself.

And sometimes focusing on the criminal-legal system seemed worth it. For example, as a member of one of our local domestic violence task forces, we worked closely with advocates to dismiss a judge who was requiring domestic violence victims to describe in detail the ways in which their partners had sexually exploited them. Our strategic response was patient and deliberate: we enlisted the support of key members of our task force, including law enforcement and prosecutors, to sign off on a letter to superior court that judge, requesting that he refrain from inappropriately interrogating victims. When he didn't, we sent a letter to the Superior Court judge Clarence Seeliger registering our concerns, our attempts to remedy them, and a request for him to not reappoint the offending judge. Within four months, that judge was no longer on the bench.

But holding the system, and particularly judges, accountable is an iffy-at-best proposition. Even implementing a safety audit system, like the groundbreaking one developed by Ellen Pence and Praxis International (an organization that developed a method of examining institutionalized sexism), doesn't speak to some ongoing, underlying problems. For example, when we finally get a judge, prosecutor, or sheriff that "gets it" and understands the importance of soliciting the advice of those who directly serve survivors, they are not only too few, they, like commanding officers, deans and preachers, move on or up in their careers to another campus, post, or congregation. And, even with the best policies and protocols in place, if "the new sheriff in town" is clueless, they won't be enforced properly, if at all.

So, I and others at MSV have felt that our movement has too often put energy and resources into a justice system that the majority of victims don't turn to, a system that will never adequately address the needs of communities marginalized by race, immigrant status, sexual orientation and class.

Perhaps MSV's strongest contribution to addressing shortcomings in the criminal-legal response has been to focus on incorporating cultural competence into policies affecting marginalized communities.

When the U.S. Department of Justice identified Men Stopping Violence as a program that was using innovative practices to work with African-American men, criminal-legal teams, including judges, defense attorneys, victims' advocates and prosecutors, were invited to attend MSV classes for African-American men to experience the work firsthand. Women attendees were invited to observe the classes, while men attendees were invited to be participant-observers who would participate, like all the other men in the room, when called upon. Our training experience informs us that men from the community gain a deeper understanding about the content when their learning process is significantly experiential.

That being said, the criminal-legal teams were invited to attend the MSV Tactics and Choices class, for men in DeKalb County, Georgia, who are required to attend a one-time, three-hour class as a condition of their bond posted for a family violence offense. Held in the jury room of the courthouse, this is the same class referred to earlier where I questioned the validity of white men facilitating a class for predominantly African-American men. And, just as in the late 80s and early 90s when I was co-facilitating the class, at least 98 percent of the men in the room were African-American in a county where, according to 2005 U.S. census figures, the county population is 56 percent African-American.

One major difference today is that the class is designed and facilitated by Sulaiman Nurridin and Ulester Douglas, who had created MSV's all African-American men's class. Besides their decades of experience in facilitating men's trainings and classes, they brought unique teaching styles into the room. Sulaiman brings a kind of street preacher-man way of engaging with men. Ulester, who at one point was considering a career in radio broadcasting, brings his deep

Caribbean-accented voice and analysis to the room. It is quite a combo and it needs to be, because those men who show up for that three-hour class are feeling resentful and victimized by a legal system they experience as stacked against black men and in favor of all women. They're typically hopping mad, because they're missing work, in trouble with the boss, scrambling to deal with child-care arrangements, embarrassed, humiliated—not happy campers.

Sulaiman welcomes them to the class, inviting them to collectively move forward (they're all seated as far back and distant from the presenters in the front of the room as they can possibly get) so they can fully participate in the experience. And participation is mandatory.

After Sulaiman has acknowledged his appreciation of the obstacles they had to overcome to get to that room in time, and after he has noted that they will not be judged or put down for how they got there, and after he has noted that they will have the rare opportunity to talk about the things that most matter to them in their lives and that their focus will be on them and not the person who requested police protection from them, he tells them that in order to get credit for the class they will have to actively participate. He will call on them or they can raise their hands but they cannot hide out for the three hours and expect to matriculate. So, he brings the carrot and the stick to a carefully structured experience.

They start by watching and processing an excerpt from the film *What's Love Got to Do With It*, the story of Tina Turner. Having established a tone of respect and clear expectations, Ulester and Sulaiman begin by addressing men's resistance to taking responsibility for their choice to be violent. To "out" the women-blaming in the room, they ask the men why they think Ike battered Tina. Their responses can be both compelling and chilling. Because, unlike a group of predominantly white men, these men tend to get honest in a hurry, not only about what Ike did and why he did it, but also about why Tina and other women deserve what they get. The facilitators illuminate the women-hating that drives the violence and respectfully deconstruct how Ike makes purposeful choices in order to control Tina and the ways those choices are devastating to Tina and their children. And then they ask the men to assist them in putting Ike on the Power and Control Wheel.

Also, as a part of defining the tactics that Ike uses to manipulate Tina, they disclose ways that they, the facilitators, have used tactics to control significant others in their lives. By then men are into it, competing to participate and be heard by the facilitators. Finally, the facilitators invite the men to put themselves on the wheel.

I don't know whether Ulester or Sulaiman ever called on any participant/observer judges to put themselves on the wheel, but they wouldn't have to. Any man sitting there contemplating the full range of tactics men use to control women will have a hard time resisting identifying their own tactics of choice. Especially since, after first sitting and reflecting, the men surrounding them break into full-blown participation, clamoring to claim their tactics.

After they are given a brief break, the men come back into the room to witness a role-play in which a man experiences being "provoked" by his partner. Faced with a number of unnerving things that she says and does the role play ends with men in the room being asked, "So, what would you do in this situation? How could you stand up for yourself without stepping on her?"

By this point the men have been fully experiencing the unique sharing of power and responsibilities between Ulester and Sulaiman, which further engenders their trust and reduces the atmosphere of competition that so often defines how men relate in groups.

Using humor, self-disclosure, contemporary and historical accounts of how men mistreat women and other men, they continually encourage the men to "get real" in the room. And, sometimes, when the men challenge the facilitators on something they experience as a contradiction in the facilitators' thinking, the facilitators mirror that concern and respectfully model a mutual learning process. During the final exercise, "The Arc of Choice," men are invited to explore how they can access their thoughts and feelings to make more constructive choices in their lives, particularly when they are faced with conflict.

The point of the Tactics and Choices class, then, is for men to experience accountability, but an accountability that is rooted in restorative rather than punitive justice. This class isn't a substitute for the state-mandated, 24-week programs to which most of these men sentenced, but it does provide men with an intense experience where they can address some of the real challenges they face in their everyday lives. An experience that encourages them to approach their six-month mandated class with at least an open mind. But accountability is the bottom line in that class and some of the men experience consequences for the choices they make while attending it. For example, it's not uncommon for Sulaiman, towards the end of the three hours, to invite men who haven't yet contributed to the discussion to offer their opinions on what they've learned so far. Kind of a last chance before the door closes. Men who don't participate and don't respond to his offer are told that they will return in two weeks to attend the next three-hour class in order to get credit for it. So, the expectations around participation are spelled out early and, when they're not met, they experience the consequences.

The take-home messages for the men in the room are not lost on the criminal-legal teams observing them. They can see that when accountability is administered with respect to men who hold little regard for the system, the results can be favorable for the perpetrator and the victim. Focusing on the meaning of his choice-making, he can take more responsibility for the consequences of his abuse and he can decide whether he will continue to hold her responsible for his being held accountable by the court. Without the carrot, the stick may do more harm than good.

I've witnessed judges treating batterers with contempt, apparently believing that a good lecturing from the bench will set them straight. I've also experienced judges colluding with the batterer, compromising victim safety by imposing inappropriate sentencing such as couples counseling, anger management and/or a short-term batterers' program for one or both. In these two cases the message is consistent: his abuse isn't that serious and both parties are responsible for the problem and for its solution. And there are also judges who know how to conduct safe and just hearings. In that regard, judges aren't that different from everyone else who's trying to figure out what to do with men who abuse women; it's just harder to find effective means for holding judges accountable.

The three-hour class teaches a condensed version of the Core Principles we teach in our six-month classes. As such, our intention is for the criminal-legal teams observing the class to come away with an experiential understanding of the efficacy of restorative justice. But we expect more than that.

Sitting in that room and listening to batterers claim their systematic use of devastating abuse is unsettling for everyone. When there are women observing the class we ask them to sit more towards the back of the room so that when the men bring their blatant misogyny, the women have the choice to stay and witness it or to excuse themselves from being further subjected to it.

We're so used to everyone, including the victim, minimizing the tactics and their effects that when the raw truth comes out we have to know how resistant we are to knowing what he does and how she survives it. Her reality, the choices she makes to pursue safety for herself and her children, begins to make more sense to all of us in the room, including the batterer, the facilitators and each member of the criminal-legal team. That team came to learn about the batterer and what to do with him. Our expectation is that they will also leave knowing more about themselves and particularly what they need to consider when adjudicating cases with men in general and particularly men of color. Our hope is that they will arrive at more just and humane determinations than the mass incarceration of men of color.

The Tactics and Choices class has been a work-in-progress for many years. One of the ways we refined it was to invite community partners in to witness the work and to comment on it. It was partly from their feedback that we chose to use that class to train criminal-legal personnel on effective interventions with African-American men. We liked to think that our analysis and practice around culture were cutting edge, but we had our share of embarrassing moments that became teachable moments. We most certainly had some lessons to learn from our "cultural incompetence."

In the early 90s, Caminar Latino, under the direction of Julia Perilla, began working with Latino families in the greater Atlanta community. They were a grassroots program based in a Catholic mission located in the heart of Atlanta's Spanish-speaking community. While we at MSV were aware of their work, we felt free to publicly question their choice to work with families in the context of the Catholic Church. We questioned their judgment to work with an iconic patriarchal institution not known for its efforts to create safe space for victims of violence. We were also alarmed by their decision to intervene with the entire family—the victim, the perpetrator, and their children—in the same location and at the same time. For us it raised all the red flags the mainstream movement had established around victim safety and the need to establish boundaries between where and when women would attend support groups and where and when men would attend batterers' intervention groups. So, while we had great respect for Julia, we persisted in our criticisms.

At one point, Kathleen called Julia to say that their choice to hold survivor support groups in the same space with their batterers would result in Latinas getting killed, imploring her to reconsider that choice. Julia's response was that her choice was based on the strong voices of the Latinas in their community, who insisted that if they didn't hold the groups in one place for the entire family, no one would attend.

Julia and her staff were never defensive with us, they simply and firmly persisted in doing what they knew was right for their community, while frequently inviting us to come to observe their work. One day, I went to the mission. When I walked in the first thing I saw was a long table filled with food: breads, fruit, vegetables, baked chickens, all brought by the families to share before they attended their groups on that Wednesday night. I was invited to share food with them and then invited to witness the men's work. Because of the frequency of co-occurrence of domestic violence and substance abuse in this population, all men were required to address both. The first hour of each two and a half hour weekly group was a substance abuse education meeting and the remaining one and one half hours was for domestic violence intervention. Even though I couldn't speak Spanish, I could understand what was being said and there were several clear messages being delivered. One, the facilitators were there as resources to guide the learning process more than as experts. Since most of the men attending were immigrants who had experienced varying forms of oppression, there was an intention to do away with unnecessary hierarchical relationships and to cultivate a climate of respect. Men who had completed the program were in the room to model and support the practice of being accountable for their abusive behaviors. I later learned that their structured groups focus on addressing the oppression in relationships that mirrors the power imbalances that are present throughout society based on class, gender, race/ethnicity, sexual orientation, abled-ness, and education. Thus, Caminar Latino draws heavily on the philosophy of Paolo Friere, renowned Brazilian educator and philosopher, using a "critical consciousness" model that includes information sharing, dialogue, and re-education components. Their curriculum is based on a culturally competent model developed and refined for the Atlanta Latino community by Antonio Ramirez Hernandez.[8]

While I saw clear demonstration of men holding men accountable, I was also aware of a conspicuous absence of a punitive tone in the room.

And then there was the priest.

Father Carlos roamed from room to room, sometimes in the room with the men, when invited, in the room with the women, and then in the room with the children, encouraging safety and accountability, blessing their commitment to creating healthy families, letting all know that the mission was a safe sanctuary for the family to do that work.

Even before I left that evening, I began to understand the truth in Julia's claim that if Caminar Latino were to offer separate services for individual family members, they would not come. They would not come because, according to their cultural traditions, any solution for the problems experienced by any individual family member would have to include the whole family.

When Spanish-speaking men would call MSV to inquire about our program we would say that we would welcome their application, and we would also mention Caminar Latino as an excellent program that, if they chose to experience Spanish-speaking facilitators, might be their preferred choice.

I can recall one Latino man who enrolled in one of our classes. He appeared to be deeply committed to the work, completing all his assignments, contacting every man in the class weekly. Near his fifth week he came into class reporting that he had gotten angry with his partner, raised his voice, and thrown an object against the wall as he was leaving their apartment. When we reminded him that, according to his signed contract, using physical force against his partner of any kind would result in his having to move out of the home, he broke into tears and begged us to let him remain in the home, saying that it was unthinkable that, as a Latino, he would abandon his family. We sympathized with his dilemma and said that we couldn't make him do anything but if he wanted to remain in the program he would have to move out. The following week he came to class to tell the men and us that he dreaded dropping out of the program but that he couldn't betray his family by moving out. I won't ever forget that man, our decision, and his.

Caminar Latino, by providing their program in the mission, encouraged the family to come together in a safe environment where they could then go their separate ways to address their individual and collective needs. The stated objective of the program

> "is not to keep the families together, as this could increase the risk to the women and the children. It is rather to provide spaces and services in which Latina battered women can gain a sense of their rights, their options, and their strengths while deciding for themselves the course of their lives."[9]

The men's program within the comprehensive intervention is designed for men to take responsibility for their abuse, to learn and practice alternative behaviors and listen to and respond to the needs of the women they have abused. So, the goals of their program were as insistent on victim safety as any other in existence. They simply go about it by drawing on cultural values that are more likely to make it happen. And this was another example where, as with the Baptist preacher who recruited participants for Because We Have Daughters', the priest used the power of his position to reinforce the take-home messages from Caminar Latino.

Having visited the mission, I had to come to terms with my own resistance to acknowledge that they knew something we didn't know. We couldn't see it because it didn't look like ours.

And then another thing happened that challenged our competence: just as Caminar Latino was setting up their batterers' group, Julia approached us to request that we train one of the men from their community to co-facilitate their group. We were flattered to be asked, but when we were told that this man had previously battered a Latina on their staff we balked, saying that we didn't believe it was appropriate for a man who had battered to be given the responsibility and the prestige of leading other men. Julia responded that this man had taken full responsibility for his abuse, had done accountability work with his partner and their organization, and was the best man they knew of to do the work. Moreover, his partner, Juana, had recommended him for the position. We went forward with her request, setting up a special internship for him. But we had real reservations and only did it because of our deep respect for Julia.

When Felipe Perez entered our internship his first step was to join one of our classes as a member. I remember him for his incredible courage, for his telling the truth of his own abuse, for confronting other men on theirs, and for his doing it with incredible care and compassion. Since he was the only Latino in the class, I wondered if men would dismiss him. But they didn't. He spoke slowly from his heart—and with an accent, which I think meant that men had to listen more carefully to hear what he had to say. It wasn't long before he became a leader in the class and once again we had to acknowledge that our theory on "the way to do it" just didn't hold up. Today, Felipe is known not only in Latino communities but also among all of us who do the work, as one of the premier instructor-trainers in the field.

Felipe and Julia weren't the only ones who challenged our cultural competence. They had mentored a young man named J.P., who facilitated batterers groups for Tapestri, an organization made up of agencies that provide domestic violence-related services to families from the international communities in Georgia. I was pleased when J.P. invited me to attend one of his groups and, not surprisingly, I had another learning moment. Soon after I sat in their circle of men, I saw that I was, with the exception of J.P., the only man for whom English was the primary language. Men were speaking in languages from all over the world and also, to the best of their abilities, they were welcoming me to their group. J.P. had already gotten their permission for me to sit in on their group so they had some idea who I was. The first thing that struck me was the deep respect with which J.P. addressed each man. He was acutely aware of the many borders and obstacles each man had had to cross to reach the United States and then the many challenges and humiliations they had experienced since arriving here.

And then came a most poignant, at least for me, moment when after the men had checked in, claiming their controlling behaviors during the previous week, they were invited to give each other feedback. The operational word here being "invited," because J.P. and every other man who offered feedback, before giving it, would ask the man to whom he was giving it if he was open to receiving it. It had never occurred to me that receiving feedback could be a choice. In our classes, generally, ready or willing or not, we give it. So, typically I would turn to a man and say, "Don, I have some feedback for you." I think we rightfully focus on the importance of maintaining a structure that confronts male privilege, emphasizing listening without interrupting and keeping agreements. But as I was sitting there in J.P.'s group, I was aware of the empowering effect of the respectful invitation on refugee and immigrant men for whom much of their experience with authorities in this country was replete with disrespect. As I was sitting there and in days following it I had to ask myself, why wouldn't I ask men in our MSV classes, before giving it, if they were open to receiving it? And even if a man said "no" to my request, it could open up opportunities for other men in the class to ask him to talk about the source of his resistance: for example, is his resistance rooted in his denial, minimization and blaming others for his abuse? Or is it coming from a place of shame, an inchoate knowing that he simply can't take in any more difficult truths at that moment? Or both?

We generally don't have time to delve deeply into men's shame in our classes, but as a psycho-educational experience we do attend to men's pain by creating space for men to model and practice self and mutual emotional nurturance. Asking a man if he's prepared to receive feedback is honoring his right and responsibility to monitor his capacity to deal with potentially painful truths. Whether in class or in life in general, that practice makes sense, and I'm still thanking J.P. and Tapestri for that simple but powerful lesson.

CHAPTER 6

Times Changed and So Did We

Then you better start swimming or you'll sink like a stone
For the times they are a-changin.

"The Times They Are A-Changin,'" Bob Dylan

O ur shift in program priorities wouldn't hold unless we "institutionalized" those priorities. Following Kathleen's death in 1996, a planning team formed to construct the future of MSV. The team was composed of board, staff, and key community partners. For most of us, it was hard to think or talk about going on without her. It was wrenching because we knew we had to do right by her legacy and we also knew that we had to do different. But as much as we stayed on task, we never let our focus get in the way our sharing raucous laughter, poignant memories, and fabulous food. She would have loved it.

Reflecting on Kathleen's thoughts before she died, the committee concluded that the organizational structure needed to address three primary concerns. Of paramount importance was the need to maintain women's role of leadership and authority, and we decided to do that in two ways: first, we incorporated in the by-laws that women would constitute a majority of the board; second, we would hire two women consultants who would monitor the work of the men. Libby

Cates Robinson and Sandra Barnhill had been operating in a version of that capacity since Kathleen's death.

The second primary concern was the need to have women and men of color assume meaningful (not token) positions of power within the organization.

The third primary concern was connected to the first. While we understood the importance of maintaining women's authority, it had become clear that men needed to assume significantly more responsibility for managing day-to-day operations. The committee endorsed Kathleen's idea that it was time for men to step up and do more of the grunt work, the maintenance work of the organization, i.e., more of the fundraising, men asking men for financial support, and more of the administrative tasks like budget management, board recruitment, and staff supervision.

She wanted men to take on program supervision, making sure that program content and delivery were congruent with our mission. And she definitely wanted men to take on more responsibility for holding men on staff accountable—accountable for how we conducted ourselves on and off the job. It was one thing for her to monitor our movement work with men and women; it was a whole other thing for her to have to monitor our running amok in our personal lives.

Over the years, there were men on staff who abused women, other men, and drugs. Through our accountability group check-ins we were once again confirming that we were not all that different from other men. Reporting our controlling and abusive behaviors towards women and other men, our excessive use of alcohol and or drugs, our racist and heterosexist thinking and behaviors were the right things for us to do.

But it had to be galling for Kathleen. Unlike many other women in the domestic violence and sexual assault movements, she was rarely surprised or shocked by what we would do or report, but it confounded her that she had to bear the burden of finding and imposing the right consequences, and then deal with the brunt of how we might react to those consequences. It was clear that the burden of holding men on staff accountable had to shift. But for men to take these things on, the planning committee decided that men needed to acquire a more formalized leadership role, to make men more responsible without authority would result in women once again cleaning up after men.

As we were deliberating on our future, I don't know what others were thinking, but I know I had a major monologue running in my head: "Man, I'm not sure who could follow Kathleen or, for that matter, who would want to. Wouldn't she get caught up in comparing herself to Kathleen? How could she not? How could we not? They say it takes a couple of hires before you really succeed an icon. So if her successor is doomed, should we just accept that and settle for whoever is willing, if not ready, to take this on?"

Nah.

I remember asking Kathleen, before she died, "What do you think we should do?"

"You'll know," she said. I acted then like I knew what she was talking about, but when I later began working with Libby, Sandra and the other women in the planning process, it was clear they weren't going to "settle." That committee was moving on the idea that it was time for a man or men to take on the leadership. And that if we were to honor the recommendations from the African-American Initiative, an African-American man or men needed to be in a leadership position.

When we thought about it, it was pretty clear that there was no one man who had the qualifications to do the job. We didn't want to set any one person up for failure, but when we came up with the possibility of sharing the responsibility with co-executive directors the committee moved closer to consensus. Ultimately they chose Ulester to be the Program Executive Director and me to be the Administrative Director. When the committee presented the idea to the board and the staff, the reaction, in my estimation, was in part relief, because after nearly a year of deliberation a decision had been made and, in part, trepidation. What would it mean to turn the leadership over to men?

Then there was also some confusion. How could these two men with no history of administering an organization be entrusted with this task?

And why me and not Gus? And why Ulester and not Sulaiman? I knew some but not all the reasoning behind the decision. Perhaps it was because we represented the best balance. Anyone who had ever experienced Ulester's training facilitation knew that he was incredibly charismatic and wise. If nothing else, I was perceived as a reliable and steadying influence.

Since Kathleen's sabbatical in 1994 and then her illness in 1995, I had been the acting executive director. So people knew what they could expect from me. My recollection is that reactions throughout the community were mixed, though generally favorable. And I also knew that there were board and staff who were really struggling with the decision. Ultimately, maybe they could go with it because they trusted the integrity of our process. The committee, led and composed primarily of women of all genders and ethnicities, represented our main community partners from the domestic violence and sexual assault communities. Our process was slow and deliberate and rooted in our Core Principles. Besides a full range of women's voices being central to our process, there was a major emphasis on community accountability. Before making the final decision, committee representatives met with key community partners to solicit their reaction to two men directing MSV. When they heard our reasoning, they admitted to feeling jolted by the shift, but understanding of the reasons and affirming of the choice. Ulester assuming a primary position of power in the organization was speaking, in a concrete way, to the concern raised by the AAI, that race matters.

And I suspect that while the committee could see our limitations, they had no doubt about our deep commitment to upholding the Core Principles, including and especially the concept of organizing men as being more important than fixing individual batterers. Ulester had not only an understanding of the concept of intersectionality, but of how essential its incorporation in our work was to our accomplishing our mission.

So there we were, a black gay man and a straight white guy, co-EDs of MSV. We were excited and not just a little humbled by the task before us. I think both of us were clearly feeling the imperative to move on our mission and particularly to address issues pertaining to race and intersectionality. The women on the planning committee expected us to move these issues from token status to organizational priority, to use our unique combination of position power and social location to put into practice Core Principles on which MSV said it stood, but on which we had too often waffled. One thing seemed likely: with Ulester as co-ED and Sulaiman as the Director of Men's Education, we would no longer be mistaken for a white-led organization.

One of the first and most difficult actions Ulester and I had to take was to fire Gus. Gus' analysis and practice were experienced in ways that were incongruous with our organizational needs going forward. And though we struggled tenaciously, meeting over several years, first in mediation sessions when Kathleen was still with us and subsequently in numerous accountability sessions, we couldn't resolve those differences. While it was clearly the right decision, I've long thought that our termination process, the way we implemented the decision, was abrupt and disrespectful to Gus. And it was way too hard for way too many people to understand and accept. We did right by getting affirmation and direction from the board and from Libby and Sandra, but on a personal level, for Gus and for us, it took a tremendous toll. I know Ulester was deeply distressed by it. For me, Gus was one of our son Sam's godparents, one of Jesse's closest friends, and one of my closest allies in the work.

If I thought that the lessons learned from this experience would override the pain that too many of us experience, even to this day, I would describe it in more detail.

For many of our allies and friends, recovering from that decision has been a long, arduous and stressful process. And I've often thought of its lingering effects. For example, I think it had some bearing on how Ulester and I held and didn't hold ourselves and other men accountable on staff. Consciously and unconsciously, I think we became careful and deliberate in our decision-making, sometimes to the point of paralysis. It was no excuse. It was just an overwhelming circumstance with which to deal.

Challenge and Reward

When Libby Cates Robinson and Sandra Barnhill were named the organizational consultants to whom Ulester and I would report for feedback and guidance on our work, there was a general sense of relief both within and without the organization.

Libby and Sandra had not only been board members, they had co-led MSV trainings. Libby had served as principal investigator for our CDC project and Sandra had been a core member of the African-American Initiative. So they both had a long history of giving us feedback on our work. The expectation was that Ulester and I would meet with Sandra and Libby to report on our administrative and programmatic decisions and their effects generally and particularly on women.

While this "accountability structure" looked good on paper, in practice it didn't always work out. At once a strength and a weakness of our leadership style, Ulester and I tended to meet and deliberate on most major matters, both administrative and programmatic. We were so intent on ensuring that we shared our power equitably that, when it came to decision making, we weighed in with each other constantly. Our intentions were good, but it was frustrating for those who were most immediately affected by our slow process, namely the staff. While Ulester and I were intentional about supportively challenging each other on how we were doing our jobs, including how we were using or misusing our power, that generally happened in private meetings with just the two of us and not in the presence of the rest of the staff. So, they never directly experienced us doing our accountability work, modeling accountability, and I think that the goal of men holding men on staff accountable was compromised.

Sandra and Libby were frustrated as well, because Ulester and I would show up at their meetings asking them to weigh in on decisions we had yet to make, instead of requesting their feedback on the decisions we had already made. They would say that we were spending too much time processing and not enough time doing. And they also expressed frustration that they had to do too much of our work with and for us.

But this transition process wasn't simple because the other part of making real institutional change meant that I needed to step back and create space for Ulester to assume his rightful and real position power. So, when one of our longtime allies would call and ask for me because they'd known me for years, I referred them to Ulester. Sometimes I was jealous, because, after all, I was a founder and had earned the right to steer them where in our organization they needed to go. But I also knew that was no longer my job. The thing I knew how to do was to step aside and create room for Ulester to lead, not because if I did so I could feel magnanimous, but because if I didn't he wouldn't have the space to show what he could do, and we would fail. It was interesting that one of the most important things I could do transform our organizational culture was to do less. It's one of the intriguing things about white male privilege. Sometime you can use it by stepping up, taking action, speaking with and for oppressed people, and sometimes you can use it by absenting yourself, becoming selectively silent when it really matters.

When we were in a room with funders or allies who knew me and would direct a question to me by their eye contact or words, I would either wait for Ulester to respond or ask him what he thought. And that wasn't because I didn't have an answer, but because I knew that not only did he know what to say, but that he would bring his unique lens and voice to the response. And it wasn't like I disappeared and relinquished my power and authority. It was more a matter of creating conditions in which we could both share in the balance of power. And there were many occasions when Ulester took the lead. For example, because of his having established a strong reputation with officials in the Department of Justice, he was the one who would intentionally defer to me so they could get some sense of how my thinking complemented his.

Alas, those transition years were challenging but also rewarding. Under incredibly stressful conditions, Red, Brian Nichols and Libby produced a highly successful completion of the five-year CDC demonstration project. We continued to provide state-of-the-art trainings, locally and nationally, receiving a three-year grant from the Department of Justice's Office on Violence Against Women (OVW) to hone our mentoring model and to provide trainings for men on how to work as allies to women. We used our classrooms as laboratories for learning how to engage with men in the community. We strengthened our internship and mentoring programs.

Ulester gained national and international acclaim by providing trainings and keynote addresses that questioned the efficacy of stand-alone batterers programs, challenging and educating communities on how to put more energy into organizing mainstream men to prevent violence against women.

And there was one initiative about which I think Ulester and I felt particularly pleased. While we had become clear about limiting the resources we put towards improving the criminal-legal system's response to domestic violence, we felt compelled to respond to the needs of thousands of women whose partners had been incarcerated in the state of Georgia.

In 1997, the Georgia Department of Corrections partnered with Men Stopping Violence to develop a family violence curriculum to be taught to all male Georgia inmates prior to their release from prison.

The 12-session curriculum included units on partner abuse, including same-sex partners, sexual assault, stalking, child abuse, and elder abuse. After writing and then testing the curriculum in focus groups, MSV provided ongoing, in-service training for prison staff that would teach the curriculum over the next 10-plus years. Gus Kaufman, Kathy Steele, Quiyama Rahman, and Vicky Elesa authored a first-class document. Not surprisingly, many of the prison staff trainees carried the same attitudes and beliefs about women as those held by the inmates. And, like the Tactics and Choices court class, where men bring their rawest truths, those in-service trainings required our best work. Much of their staff was unaware of the levels of trauma that they were dealing with, not only in the prison population, but also within themselves.

Think about prison rape, the effects it has on the survivor and everyone around him or her, including the staff, and you have some idea of the nature and intensity of those in-service sessions.

Ulester and I, who provided the bulk of those trainings, were constantly improvising to accommodate the pressing issues brought forward by their staff. Yvonne Saunders Brown, the Program Development Coordinator for the state and county Department of Corrections, and a tenacious advocate for justice, fought for this curriculum to be available system-wide. She understood how important it was for their staff to help inmates prepare for the massive transition they would undergo from prison to family and community life. I like to believe that we partnered with her to support thousands of men through that process.

One of my greatest challenges as co-ED was fundraising, and particularly increasing the number of men who would support our work. Kathleen, before her death, had created a Development Council, which consisted of men with influence and affluence who had completed our 24-week program and who were meeting with her quarterly to strategize how to increase funds by increasing the number of men who would contribute money for our work.

But of course, as has been said many times throughout MSV's history, "no good deed goes unpunished." One of our most influential Development Council members, a high-ranking corporate executive, turned out to be a man who, following his completion of our program and while he was claiming to make amends with his partner, was discovered conducting an online affair with a woman in another state, a woman for whom he eventually left his partner and two children.

While Kathleen was on her six-month writing sabbatical in California, she sent a video message to the Development Council at the end of which she made her memorable exhortation for those men to stand up for justice. Referring to the role of white men in the 1995 terrorist bomb attack on the federal building in Oklahoma City, Kathleen inspired the council with the following words:

"What the Oklahoma bombing has done for me is to bring me face-to-face with how deep the resistance is to real liberty for women, people of color and gays and lesbians. In its manifestation of opposing the government, the BFT, federal agents, their resistance looks like it is men fighting other men (after all the only worthy opponents). But this battle among men is taking place on a field of women, people of color, gays and lesbians. The government in this scenario is code language for the rights of others, others who are supposed only to serve them and remain subordinate to men, to whites, white men. The lines are being drawn.

And so it seems to me really crucial that the question be raised. Where does men's interest lie? Is it in more and more oppression and repression, more control, more exaggerated hyper-masculinity that gains its force from the hatred of women and all others who are different? Or is it in making justice? Who is going to say that men's self-interest lies in making justice? Where in the public discussion is this question going to get raised? What each of you will be doing as you go out to build support for MSV is really to serve a much larger objective than simply to gain support of our organization. It's really to raise in the public consciousness the question, 'Where does men's interest lie?' And then from that place inside of you that has learned it in a very personal way, talk to men about how, in fact, their self-interest lies within a society where justice prevails."

So, Kathleen was firing up her council not to just go out and get money for MSV, but to mobilize men around justice-making. All of us, including men on staff, were stirred by her message. But by then Kathleen had contracted cancer and that group of men never met with her again.

During my tenure as Co-ED, I attempted to revive the Development Council, but I was mostly interested in those men raising money for MSV. So often it had been women as individual donors, as board members of corporations and foundations, who would get and give money to MSV. I certainly didn't want to tamper with that. I just wanted men in similar positions to do the same thing. I think the rationale for recruiting men who had been through our 24-week program was, as Kathleen noted, that they understood the personal benefits of that experience and would be motivated to raise money for our work. But, clearly, I was missing something here. I sometimes wondered if part of what discouraged them from actively and publically promoting and fundraising for our work is that it tapped into their shame and caution around the possibility that they would be identified as or associated with men who abuse women. It's not a feel-good give or get for men, because it reminds us all of what men do to women.

My Development Council initiative fizzled after about a year. It might have been because I brought the wrong attitude to it. Unlike in classes where I expected men to show up and do the work and they did, I think I felt and expressed too much gratitude for the men who said they would go out and solicit money for MSV. I didn't expect enough. I didn't specifically ask for much and they didn't produce. I didn't use the direct "ask," where I might say something like, "Having heard our smart goals and objectives for our mentoring project, will you two men (from the council) go out and raise $10,000 so we can train three men to mentor 30 high school boys?" And then shut up until they answered yes, no, or why not.

But something important was happening at the same time. I was beginning to see fundraising as an opportunity to explain our work and to grow the number of men and women who would support out mission. In the early 2000s we initiated our "Making Waves" gatherings in which individuals and couples who were already strong supporters would invite friends to attend a dessert or wine and cheese party to hear an MSV rep tell about our work and ask for their support. We clearly increased our number of individual donors, and they had a much clearer concept of how they could support us in financial and non-financial ways. Of course, we asked for both, but in the non-financial ways we offered them choices, like inviting us to present in their workplaces and faith communities. We also spelled out specific ways they could intervene when they become aware of a situation in which a man is abusing a woman. By then we had reworked our manual (*A Conversation, Men: What You Can Say and Do to Make a Difference*), on what men can say or do when confronted with domestic violence. Our experience in talking with men about their options is that they are generally much clearer about why *not* to intervene, quickly listing the bad things that would happen to her, to him and to them, when making that choice. Providing practical doable options, the manual makes a compelling case and it provided us with the content for some terrific exchanges during out Making Waves gatherings.

So, while I got clearer about how to increase and educate our supporters, they were most often like-minded progressives with big hearts and small pockets. Our big fund-raisers were well attended and great at inspiring our base, but not particularly successful at generating income. I remember more than one savvy nonprofit E.D., when hearing our annual budget total around $500,000-plus saying, "Wow, given who you are as an organization, how long you've been here and what you've accomplished, I would think your budget would easily exceed a million."

At our 20th anniversary celebration, we had a raucous and wonderful time at the Carter Center, toasting and roasting the many remarkable people who had brought us to that point. In the course of that evening we more than once took some heavy and humorous shots at the Bush Administration, which stirred mostly thunderous applause. But just one problem with that choice: some of our most loyal and long-term supporters in the room were Republicans who had felt deeply committed to our mission, but equally affronted by our reckless willingness to insult their politics. Subsequently, as Administrative E.D., I was appropriately confronted by one those supporters, and while I learned an important lesson about when and where to energize supporters without engaging in partisan rhetoric, I was also reminded of how naïve I was to the ways of cultivating and sustaining important donors. Ideally, we would have balanced our small progressive gatherings with larger celebratory events more geared to attracting and consolidating lucrative support.

It's important to dwell on the funding aspects of our history because, like many nonprofits, there were moments when, because we'd come close to not making our budget, we had to release or reduce time for some very dedicated and talented staff. I hated this part of the work and it's one of the reasons why Ulester and I were ready to relinquish our roles after six years as Co-E.Ds. At best, I did a poor job of relating to our board and they were equally relieved when Ulester and I elected to step back and become staff members again, where we could bring our best strengths to the work.

But before that transition, towards the end of our term as Co-E.D.s, after several years of supporters and allies urging us to upgrade our physical plant, we finally found a suitable site at 533 W. Howard Ave. in Decatur, Georgia.

Our search for a new space had some memorable moments. In the early stages, Dolly Evans, one of our long-term allies and supporters, was adamant about our locating in a newer facility, and she once remarked to Ulester and me, "You know, I don't generally return to an office that has no running hot water in the restroom."

I also recall how resistant some of our board members were to taking on an increase in our rent. The Inman Park Methodist Church, from whom we had rented for the first 12 years, felt positive about our mission and had been generously charging us relatively little for our space. One night, to bring our board around, I extended a last-minute invitation to two board members to come observe our Monday night class. It was pouring rain and coming into the classroom the first thing they saw was several wastebaskets strategically placed to capture the water dripping from a variety of leaks in our ceiling. One was actually cascading from a non-functioning light fixture in the corner of the room. That experience apparently erased any lingering doubts about our need to move and within a year we located and moved into a new space. During that last year of our term as EDs, two significant things happened: one, funding for our OVW grant was finally formally approved so we could get on with some of our more innovative prevention programs; and, two, we worked closely with our board to recruit and hire our amazing successor, Shelley Serdahely. There was, of course, considerable speculation about the meaning of hiring a new E.D. to supervise a staff that included two former Co-E.D.s, one of whom was a co-founder.

Shelley

There were a couple of things Ulester and the board and I were in complete agreement on. We were in favor of hiring a woman as ED, someone with a successful history as an ED, who could oversee both the program and administrative sides of the work, who had a proven record in development and, of course, someone with a clear history in and understanding of the Battered Women's Movement. Someone who would feel comfortable and compelled by our mission. I recall our getting a lot of strong applications, but at one point we decided to pursue a candidate who hadn't submitted an application.

Shelley Serdahely was then the executive director of the Jeanette Rankin Foundation, which provides grants to low-income women, age 35 and older, enrolled in a college or vocational training program. She was, by all accounts, happy with her position with the Rankin Foundation and had no apparent interest in pursuing the directorship at MSV. But Shelley had served as a board member and chair at the Women's Resource Center (WRC) in DeKalb County and Jean Douglas, WRC's executive director and one of our closest community partners, suggested she apply. Ulester and I had experienced Shelley facilitating trainings and delivering keynotes and we were excited by the prospect of her candidacy. As it turned out, Shelley was the last of the finalists our board-staff hiring committee interviewed and our energy was apparently flagging because soon after completing the interview she withdrew her application, saying that she didn't get the feeling that we really wanted what she would bring to MSV and that it was extremely important that, if she were to leave her current position, she would need to feel like it was the right match.

Ulester and I immediately pursued her, acknowledging her concerns, assuring her that our committee was very excited by her qualifications, asking that she reconsider her decision to withdraw. She did, and the rest is history. But that process is indicative of how exacting Shelley is about how she needs things to be. She's not rigid but she's dogged about upholding the principles on which she believes the work must stand. A survivor herself, she had already spent 30 years in the movement as a staunch ally and advocate for battered women. Jean Douglas once said of Shelley, "(For her, sic) the personal is still political and social change is as much about what you do as it is about what you say and how you live. Again and again she has been the lone voice saying what must be said no matter how hard or risky, the self-designated spokesperson against complicity."

I think Shelley was intrigued by the opportunity to mobilize men to work in the interest of women. By her report, she had spent most of her movement years working with and for women, but not directly with men. I don't know what that huge shift meant for her, but I noticed that our staff was highly motivated to work with and for her. And as much as there were questions about whether it would be possible or even advisable for her to supervise two former Co-EDs, that too seemed not so hard for all three of us.

Shelley has acknowledged that after Ulester and I implored her to continue her candidacy she was pretty clear that we wanted her to lead. That, and MSV's history of embracing the importance of women in leadership, dispelled most concerns she might have had about our undermining her authority. She noted that there was a way in which she felt that, unlike a man if he had taken the position, she could make decisions, move us forward and make mistakes and still be supported. She felt that having us on her staff was an advantage because, having held her position, we might be more likely, if not qualified, to give her useful feedback on how she was doing her work. And, she had an inclination to move quickly in her decision-making, as she would put it, a style of ready, fire, aim. She would, therefore, sometimes look to us to slow her process down. On the other hand, there were times when she felt less free to be as demanding of us as she was with other staff. She noted that she thought of us as has having earned the right to do what we did the way we did it and, for that reason, there were times when she held us to a different standard.

Meanwhile, Ulester and I were pretty thrilled to get back to doing full time program work and staff morale, in general, was soaring. I think one thing that made the whole transition seem relatively seamless was Shelley's apparent ease in relating to, working with, and supervising men of color. My take was that, as a white woman, she had done her personal homework around her racism to the point where she seemed willing and able to be direct with her expectations of men, regardless of their race and ethnicity. Shelley was and is good at reading people's strengths and then empowering them to use them.

Not that it wasn't challenging because, like all the women who worked with us, our sexism would surface soon and often enough. Though she had her share of struggles with holding us accountable, that didn't seem to curb her energy and her expectations, and that inspired us.

Among the first Core Principles Shelley embraced, was her commitment to prioritize organizing men in general over fixing men in batterers' groups. She observed that we were already adept at mobilizing movement men, men who we already committed to doing social justice work, to address the oppression of women. Shelley wanted to add the dimension if not shift our focus to men who had relatively little exposure to our work. Mainstream men in general and, in particular, men with influence and affluence.

When Shelley came to MSV she had already been questioning the wisdom of allocating so many resources towards addressing the flaws in the criminal-legal system and she was eager to create alternatives that would have better and more lasting results for all women, including battered women. She was particularly drawn to exploring prevention strategies. MSV's BWHD program, one of her most innovate inventions, is an example of how we connect with men by appealing to their own best interests. Men don't ordinarily ponder or flinch when it comes to acting on behalf of their daughters. As noted earlier, the point of this program is for men to have an experience with their daughters that would encourage them to see the importance of acting on behalf of all daughters, not just their own. Sitting in circles talking about the challenges their daughters face on a daily basis, they could recognize the need to transform the culture that compromises their daughters' sense of security and safety. And for some, they could see how connecting with or supporting MSV was a meaningful way to do that. I remember asking a man who had completed our 24-week program why he wanted to stay connected with MSV. He said something like, "I've come to realize that I just like being around MSV men, not just the class facilitators like Lee and Sulaiman, but with my classmates as well. I want to be associated with men who are doing the right thing, who are doing something to stop this war on women."

So, Shelley figured we needed to increase the number of ways men could access MSV, ways that men could connect with MSV without going through the one of our 24-week classes or our rigorous Internship Program. She understood that for men to feel good about the connection we needed to address the stigmatization issue, i.e., the idea that if you're associated with MSV you're either an abuser or a "man-hater." To change that perception, she created the True Ally Award, presented at MSV's Annual Awards Dinner to men who have dedicated time and resources to fostering safety and justice for women. Recipients have included Vice President Joe Biden, actor-singer Tim McGraw, social justice activist Paul Kivel, actor and author Hill Harper, and entrepreneur/philanthropist, George McKerrow. Each of these men has put their national notoriety and resources on the line to stand with battered women. Recognizing them offered a way for men to see that men with influence and or affluence are doing the right thing and, therefore, so could they.

To reinforce and expand the concept of true allies, Shelley, in conjunction with George McKerrow, created the True Ally Breakfast, where men from Atlanta's civic, academic, faith, and business communities meet every other month to become educated on ways they can prevent violence against women.

When Shelley first approached George, he told her frankly, "Usually when people like you talk to people like me it's when you want money. What about educating us so that we can become change agents in the world?"

Men attend these breakfasts because there is something self-affirming about being associated with a group of men who stand up and speak out about doing the right thing. As they expand their awareness of the kinds and prevalence of violence against women, they become motivated to make a difference. In large and small group discussions, they learn about the controlling tactics men use and practical strategies for addressing them.

This breakfast picks up where Kathleen's Development Council left off. Shelley would say that the Development Council was asked to give or get money so we could do the work. The True Allies *are* the work, in the sense that they bring their influential voices to communities where we've not had access. George was willing to use his profile as a highly successful businessman, business partner to Ted Turner, to recruit men for the True Ally Breakfasts. It expands its membership recruitment beyond men who have completed the MSV program to include all men. True Ally men are featured in MSV website profiles in which they speak to their commitment to empowering women to move freely and safely through the world. The core eight-man steering committee agrees to meet consistently and to bring new men to each of the bimonthly breakfasts.

While writing checks to MSV is not the focus of the meetings, men are invited to sponsor tables at the annual MSV awards dinner. They are also invited to explore ways that they can bring the fruits of their new understanding to their home and work lives. Hence, the incentive for them to become advocates and educators in the workplace, in their faith communities, their civic organizations. It remains to be seen whether men with considerable influence and or affluence will not only "buy into" our mission, but also engage in the grunt work of soliciting money to support our work.

Growing out of our commitment to reach out to all men and consistent with our Core Principle that organizing is more important than "fixing" men, Shelley and our staff began to concentrate on ways that our classroom curriculum could become more relevant and accessible to all men.

CHAPTER 7

Intersectionality Matters: Connecting the Dots

The limits of tyrants are prescribed by the endurance of those whom they oppress.

Letter to an American Slavery Abolitionist,
Frederick Douglas (1849)

Dealing with multiple and simultaneously occurring oppressions has, more often than I would like to admit, provided us opportunities to address some interesting gaps in our analysis and our practice. Sometimes that opportunity would occur when we would resist dealing with an issue around homophobia or race because of a fear that we would undermine our mission to address men's violence against women and the sexism underlying it.

For example, when we went to set up our accountability groups, we intentionally started by establishing a group for men on staff to deal with our own sexism. Then we realized that we needed to deal with our racism, then our homophobia, and so on. Each group was intentionally set up separately, presumably because that way members of the dominant group wouldn't have to call on those that they marginalized to do the grunt work of pointing out the ways that individuals and the organization itself were oppressing them.

That sequential process of setting up the separate groups revealed the hierarchy in which we viewed and dealt with oppressions.

Eventually, after consistent feedback from those who were experiencing multiple oppressions, we began to see how their experience was fragmenting and dehumanizing. So, for an African-American woman to participate in a group addressing homophobia, what was she to say or do about her experience as a woman and as an African-American? And for a black gay man to participate in the accountability group on sexism, what was he to say or do about his experience as a gay African-American? Separating the focus of each of those groups silenced the full experience of multiply oppressed participants and it particularly deprived us from learning from those who are multiply oppressed how oppressions reinforce one another.

I can remember two issues that surfaced in the heterosexism accountability group, the first of which was brought to us by Matthew Stewart, a gay white man who was an administrative assistant on staff. He pointed out that we should consider whether the climate at MSV was gay affirmative or friendly. Did the images, photos, art on our office walls reflect an interest in gay and lesbian life? Did our social conversations around "the water cooler" and at lunch breaks reflect an interest and curiosity in gay and lesbian life? He also questioned whether since some men in our classes were gay but not necessarily "out," were we establishing a culture in which they could feel safe to be true to themselves and to others?

When it came to addressing homophobia in our classes, I remember saying something to myself like, "These guys in our classes are really going to struggle to see the relevance of addressing homophobia in our classes—seeing any connection between homophobia and their mistreatment of women, the ways that homophobia reinforces sexism." And then I can recall wondering if the question of relevance was coming from the men in the class or whether it was coming from me. So, we reread Susan Pharr's article "Homophobia, A Weapon of Sexism," and held a board-staff workshop on homophobia, inviting activist Craig Washington, then on the staff of SONG, Southerners on New Ground, to facilitate didactic and experiential exercises for us to identify and understand our attitudes and beliefs around our heterosexism.

One thing I began to see was that waiting for the issue of homophobia to surface in class discussions was indicative of our halfhearted commitment to proactively draw its connection to sexism. It wasn't until we incorporated it into the lesson plans of our current curriculum, *Men At Work*, that we put our practice in better alignment with our analysis.

But, if addressing intersectionality was really to become a Core Principle of our mission, we had to make it more consistently present throughout the fabric of our work. Our trainings were a clear opportunity for making that happen.

One reason our trainings have been compelling is because we often push participants to examine how core beliefs shape the way we respond to survivors and batterers. People would usually come to our trainings to acquire nuts and bolts skills so they could work with batterers. But we would say up front that knowing your conscious and unconscious beliefs and biases will be key to your effectiveness no matter who you're working with.

Often we would begin our trainings with an experiential exercise that would facilitate participants' understanding of battered women's reality. Typically we would present them a hypothetical story of a battered woman's experience and then ask them how they would respond to her.

For example: Maria has been battered by her partner Jack who is in his third week in a family violence intervention program (FVIP). When he last physically beat Maria she sought refuge at the home of her friend, Anna. Maria had already gone to her pastor for guidance, noting to him that she has stopped coming to church because of what Jack might do if he finds her there, and telling him that since she is staying with Anna, he's threatening to have the children taken away, accusing her of being lesbian. She's asking her pastor if he'll speak to Jack. She calls Jack's FVIP facilitator and tells him that since he's been in the program Jack has physically beaten her and has been calling her and threatening to have their children taken away by "the authorities" because she has exposed them to her "lesbian" relationship with Anna. She tells the facilitator that he can't mention any of this to Jack because of what he might do to her.

The task is for the participants in the room to decide what the pastor and the facilitator should say or do with the information they have gotten from Maria. Participants break into two groups for 15 minutes to come up with strategies, which they will then report back to the large group. So, everyone is trying to figure how to help Maria without putting her at greater risk. Does the pastor call Jack in for a lecture? Does he tell Anna he wants them both to come in for a pastoral session? Does he preach a sermon on accountability? Does the facilitator challenge Jack to start bringing in reports of controlling behaviors, since he's not done so yet? Does the facilitator invite the men to talk about how they use their children to control their partners? Do the pastor and/or the facilitator call an advocate to gather input on safety measures for her? What are the possible consequences for their proposed interventions?

There's usually a lot of energy in the room when, towards the end of their processing, Ulester would ask whether, when thinking about her needs, the participants had made any assumptions about Maria's race or ethnicity. Usually some had, and some hadn't. My recollection is that most participants, regardless of their own race or ethnicity, thought of her as white. Ulester would then ask, if she were African-American, would your response to her needs be different? And if she were Latina, South Asian, or an immigrant, would you respond differently?

Not surprisingly, the group would begin to consider a whole new set of challenges when considering her race and ethnicity, or "legal status." There would be questions about her income, her job status, support from her extended family, resistance to calling the police, immigrant status, deportation, and homophobia in the church. Before asking about her ethnicity and race, the participants were mainly addressing the sexist oppression she faced as a woman. When introducing race and ethnicity it opened up the way many battered women are faced with multiple forms of interconnecting oppressions and that if we fail to see them and how they reinforce each other, we will fail her. It was from this understanding that we formally adopted the Core Principle, **"Intersectionality Matters."**

Kimberle Crenshaw, feminist, sociologist, and theorist, began writing about intersectionality in the early '90s when she was explaining the race and gender dimensions of violence against women of color. In her article, "Mapping the Margins: Intersectionality, Identity Politics and Violence Against Women of Color," she illuminates the failure of feminists to connect the experiences of gender and racial oppression:

"Feminist efforts to politicize experiences of women and antiracist efforts to politicize experiences of people of color have frequently proceeded as though the issues and experiences they each detail occur on mutually exclusive terrains. Although racism and sexism readily intersect in the lives of real people, they seldom do in feminist and antiracist practices. And so, when the practices expound identity as woman or person of color as an either /or proposition, they relegate the identity of women of color to a location that resists telling."[10]

To me that means that categorical identities such as race, gender, class, etc., don't act independently of one another, but intersect in ways that systematically discriminate against those who carry those identities. So, in the circumstances of the aforementioned Maria, as an African-American woman, she might be dealing, at a minimum, with the combined forces of racism, sexism, and homophobia.

Eventually we settled on a deconstruction of the Anita Hill/ Clarence Thomas case, incorporating it in many of our national trainings. Showing excerpts from a PBS documentary about the 1991 confirmation hearings for Thomas's Supreme Court nomination, in which Ms. Hill alleged that Thomas sexually harassed her when he was the head of the Equal Employment Opportunity Commission, the training focuses on how some of the African-Americans interviewed for the film were clear that they thought that any possible sexism suffered by Anita Hill should be subordinated to concerns about possible racism suffered by Clarence Thomas. The work of the participants in the training was to discover the ways in which intersecting oppressions get prioritized and or ignored and at whose expense that happens. Inevitably, the conversation would turn towards the meaning of an all-white male panel of senators interrogating Anita Hill, deciding whether she was telling the truth. I recall thinking what a totally untenable position she was in as an African-American woman, publically pursuing her justice as a woman, which was simultaneously being experienced as a profound betrayal of black men by many in the African-American community.

The Tactics and Choices court class was another of the places where we challenged men, in this case mostly African-American men, to unpack the intersection of racism and sexism. To help men in the classroom consider the relationship between sexism and other oppressions, we use an exercise in which we begin by asking men to cite negative messages they have heard about women. Once we have a substantial list of negative messages, we label this list "Gender Prejudice." We then invite men to name some of the powerful institutions in this country that set the norms for the socialization of men and women (government, media, religion, etc.). When we think of who is responsible for how these powerful institutions are created and operated, we see that most are run or governed by white males.

We present the men in the class with the equation: Gender Prejudice + Power = Sexism. Once men are clear about definition, we change part of the equation. We change the word "gender" to "race" and then ask men how this change affects the list of negative messages that was developed about women.

Men begin to realize that the list of messages can also be applied to their experiences with race prejudice; there is little difference between most of the negative messages about women that men hear and internalize and the negative messages about black people that white people hear and internalize.

When we now look at the list of powerful institutions, again we see that white men are responsible for establishing and operating these institutions. Thus, we have created a new equation: Race Prejudice + Power = Racism.

For many African-American men, it is the first time they have considered that their treatment of women is an act of oppression comparable to their treatment by racists. And, for all men and women in the room, it is a moment when they can see how African-American women are discriminated against by their race and their gender, and how the two together can compound her experience of oppression in devastating ways.

Seen in this light, understanding intersectionality isn't just an interesting intellectual exercise, but a practice that is essential to addressing violence against women who are oppressed in multiple ways. Hence our Core Principle: **"Intersectionality Matters."**

CHAPTER 8

A Model for Change

It's been too hard living, but I'm afraid to die
'cause I don't know what's up there, beyond the sky
it's been a long, a long time coming
but I know a change 'gon come,
Oh, yes it will.

Sam Cook, "A Change is Gonna Come"

As people in general and within organizations, locally and nationally, became more aware of our community-centered approach, we began to get requests for workshops and trainings that would explain the why and how of our programs, particularly our new curriculum, our Community Restoration Program, Because We Have Daughters', and our online Mercury internship. For our part, we were highly motivated to develop an instrument or model that would spell out how our practice and programs directly stem from our analysis. We decided on an ecological model that would explicate our understanding of the function and effects of global patriarchal violence and our approach to community-accountability strategies for confronting it.

The nature of patriarchal violence, what it is and how it works, is dense stuff. Because of its importance to us as an instrument of instruction and at the risk of lapsing into the academic, I've chosen to summarize our ecological Community-Accountability Model here.

Our definition of patriarchy is drawn from one that activist/author bell hooks espouses in her book *The Will to Change: Men, Masculinity and Love* (2003). There she describes patriarchy as

> "a political-social system that insists that males are inherently dominating, superior to everything and anyone deemed week, especially females, and endowed with the right to dominate and rule over the weak and to maintain that dominance through various forms of psychological terrorism and violence."[11]

Ecological models are known for illustrating the multiple effects and interrelatedness of social elements in an environment. In the Men Stopping Violence Community-Accountability Model we examine global patriarchy as a political-social system that is sustained and strengthened by smaller, related systems at the individual, familial, local, national, and global levels. MSV's analysis focuses on the roles of these interconnected community systems in both socializing men and reinforcing patriarchal male behaviors. But it also demonstrates how community systems themselves can be the means by which to confront patriarchal violence.

The model graphically depicts five levels of community influence (see figure 1): the individual, the primary community, the micro community, the macro community, and the global community. The individual male, his actions, and the forces that act upon him are represented by the smallest ellipse in the model. The primary community is that group just outside of the individual, consisting of his family of origin, school friends, clubs, gangs, or any group that fulfills a familial role. Beyond this is the micro community (faith communities, school systems, civic groups, social service agencies);

142

the macro community (religion, governments, mass media, high level courts such as the U.S. Supreme Court, corporations); and the global community (patriarchy and colonialism).

The arrows indicate the flow of energy and influence among these communities and how they act upon each other and how actions at each level influence the other levels. Energy and influence flow not only from the global community through smaller levels down to the individual, but also in the opposite direction; actions that occur in each community have the potential to affect change in other communities or to maintain the status quo.

The patriarchal culture system upheld by interactions between communities ensures that boys and men encounter powerful messages establishing male supremacy as the historical and cultural norm. Men and boys of every race, nationality, ethnicity, class, and sexual orientation internalize the notion of male privilege and use it in their everyday lives. Major and minor norm-setting institutions send explicit messages to boys and girls, men and women, about the superiority of men. Girls and women also internalize the message that male dominance is an established norm that must either be accepted or resisted, and neither choice ensures a woman's safety from male violence.[12]

MSV's live presentation of this model is dynamic and compelling. Participants are frequently invited to fill in the interrelated components of the model. So, for example, when the facilitator talks about the function of the primary community as that of nurturing rigid gender role conformity he/she will ask participants to identify what primary group(s) in men's lives take on that responsibility. Invariably they come up with examples that include family of origin, peers, sports teams and fraternities, often spelling out how each group goes about fulfilling its role.

This tells us that people know many of the elements of patriarchal violence. They just don't know how each element compliments and re-enforces others to seamlessly and systematically maintain patriarchal norms and, particularly, men's subordination of women. This is what the model provides for them.

But the model also exposes the irresistible but futile strategy of focusing on fixing individual men. After identifying the form and function of each succeeding community, it becomes clear that meaningful strategies have to begin and end with holding each of those communities that shape and maintain individual men, accountable. So, whether we're presenting the model to researchers at the CDC, the national college of prosecuting attorneys, university faculty and administrators, interdenominational and civic leaders, administrators or grantees from the Office on Violence Against Women, our purpose is to move leaders from micro and macro communities to see the ways that they can take action to hold the communities in their sphere of influence accountable.

But we know from experience that for many in the room it's daunting to take on entrenched institutions like the government, mass media, and faith communities. So, referring to the reverse arrows on the chart, our facilitators will talk about CRP, men who participated in the 24-week class and became eligible to assist us in education and policy work. Men on the graphic who fit in the "individual" category who, using their personal experience of transformation, take on the challenge of educating legislators regarding laws that will help or harm battered women.

Another distinguishing quality of the MSV model is that where other ecological models emphasize identifying risk factors (such as an individual's history of alcohol and drug abuse or a personal history of violence) as a way to determine the causes of violence and, therefore, the most effective strategies for intervention, the MSV model focuses on the function of each of the socializing systems as a way to identify strategies for intervention and prevention at both the individual and the cultural level. Thus, it becomes clearer that if, for example, those institutions of the micro community represent the gatekeepers who enforce the socializing messages of the primary community, it's hard to imagine the possibility of altering individuals behaviors without addressing those enforcers.

One of the more interesting opportunities for presenting the model took place when MSV contracted with Emory University in Atlanta to teach a course entitled "Intimate Partner Violence: Critical Issues and Concepts." Students from cross disciplines signed up for the course, including students from the Institute for Liberal Arts, Women and Gender Studies and African American Studies. We were particularly excited by the prospect of teaching the curriculum to men from the community at large who were not identified as batterers. We would find out whether the material we had been teaching the men in our 24-week program would be as relevant to male students on a university campus. The class offered even more interesting challenges since there were women who signed up for the course—and most of the experiential exercises in the manual were designed for men to participate in them. It meant that Ulester, who was teaching the course, had to tweak those experiences so that women could fully participate in them.

But besides this challenge, the course offered an interesting mix of learning experiences, including three different lessons from the *Men At Work* manual, guest lecturers from MSV's Community Restoration Program and from the Women's Resource Center, and an observation of a live three-hour Tactics and Choices class in the courthouse. These students got to experience an in-depth and sometimes raw look at intimate partner violence, including witnessing men at varying stages of their work to become accountable and women advocates bringing the truth of the humiliating process women go through when pursuing safety and justice.

In the Tactics and Choices courtroom class men were not only describing their controlling behaviors, they were demonstrating them in the room, sometimes trashing women by blaming them and labeling them as the true perpetrators of violence, sometimes taunting and interrupting each other in the room. In many ways it was similar to experiences of the judges and prosecutors who witnessed the class described earlier.

But this experience featured one major difference: before going into the courtroom with men and meeting with the advocates from the Women's Resource Center, these students were introduced to the lesson in the manual which features MSV's Community-Accountability model. As they rigorously studied the micro, macro, and global communities they came to a deeper understanding of how men and women at the individual level are socialized to experience intimate partner violence as "normative." The most resounding response from the students at the completion of the course was how the accountability model helped them deconstruct and understand what they had previously experienced in academic courses as dry academic theory, because they could see the theory in practice.

Patriarchal Violence

The master's tools will never dismantle the master's house.

Audre Lourde

The seventh and probably the most comprehensive Core Principle reads: "Patriarchal violence must be addressed." This principle bookends with "Women's voices are central to the work" and it is the glue that connects all the Core Principles (i.e. "Race Matters," "We Are the Work," "Community Accountability," etc.). Patriarchy and its violent means of enforcement generate the need for actualizing all of the other principles. Since every form of oppression is shaped, if not driven, by patriarchy, addressing it is an all day, every day, every-where proposition. The MSV Community-Accountability Model graphically depicts the linkage between patriarchy and its influence over the functions of the macro, the micro and the primary communities that instruct, enforce, and socialize us in adopting patriarchal behaviors and strategies.

To get at these connections it's useful to take a brief look at the form(s) and function(s) of patriarchal violence. How it works. How well it works. And for whom it works. One of the better definitions I've heard for "patriarchy" was put forth by David Potter during the Emerge conference that Gus and I attended in Ashland Mass in 1982. My recollection is that David characterized patriarchy as when a select group of Euro-American males convene in a private setting where they proceed to make decisions for and about the rest of the known world.

As the "deciders," they determine who governs and who doesn't, what's lawful and what's criminal, moral and immoral, healthy and sick, true and false, profitable and profligate. With all this in place the foot soldiers in the field, the socializers, the gatekeepers, and the enforcers, can be relied upon to carry out their responsibilities seamlessly. To look at the forms of patriarchy we need look no further than those norm-setting institutions that have shaped the socio-political-cultural landscape of the United States over the past century—and particularly who has assumed the power positions in those institutions, the people with position power to move what will be done and how it will be enforced.

So, for starters, in the United States most presidents, preachers, college presidents, and CEOs are and have been men. In a country where women represent approximately 51 percent of the population, only men have occupied the presidency, and, since the first U.S. Congress in 1789, women have held 2.2 percent of the seats in the House and the Senate. Men are currently governors of 44 of the 50 states and mayors of 92 percent of our largest cities. Interestingly, the United States ranks 69th in the world in terms of women's participation in national legislative bodies. Of the 500 largest corporations in this country, 18 or 3.6 percent are headed by women. One in 10 of those corporations have no women on their boards. Twenty-three percent of college presidents are women with twice as many men holding tenure as women. Since 1942, there have been 16 administrative directors of the CDC, one of whom was a woman. Of the past 30 presidents of the American Psychological Association, seven have been women. I couldn't find stats on this but I'm thinking most priests, pastors, preachers, rabbis, imams, and monks in this country are fellas. This is not a rigorously researched survey. I mostly went to Wikipedia for my numbers. And I didn't break down the numbers of women of color compared to white women, but where I did the numbers of women of color are relatively few. Mostly this survey reminds us who are running things now and who's been running things for a long time. This is about the patriarchs David Potter referred to: the purveyors of governance, health, pedagogy, morality, and profitability.

One of the reasons patriarchal violence has been so successful and worked so well for those who benefit from it is the various ways that its mere existence has been denied, minimized, and normalized. For example, the seventh Core Principle essentially asserts that patriarchal violence, which includes sexual and domestic violence, is used to maintain male supremacy. And, if we let ourselves take in the CDC statistics on the prevalence of male violence against women (one in three women worldwide will experience some form of physical violence at the hands of her partner during her lifetime) or the daily media reports on the terrorist assaults on women—stalking, rapes, trafficking, beatings, murders—way too often by the partners or ex-partners of the women victims, and way too often in the presence of their children, and way too often resulting in men committing homicide/suicides, killing her, their kids, and himself—why is it that we don't collectively and publicly go nuts when these atrocities keep happening? Is it because it happens so much it's come to just seem normal? Is it because we've reached the thinking that now that we have so many more women in the workforce, so many more women pursuing higher degrees, so many more women in political positions of power, so many more women competing in the Olympics, we've reached a kind of "post-sexist" world? It's reminiscent of the massive denial within white communities about the continued existence of racism, the idea that the civil rights movement, affirmative action and subsequent legislation took care of all that. That having a black man as president proves that we have moved beyond race in the United States. That we have reached a "post-racial" society.

One of the more persistent efforts to minimize the extent and effects of male violence against women has come from the field of psychology. Murray Strauss and Donald Dutton are two proponents of the "mutual combatant" theory that professes that in incidents of domestic violence, women are violent as often and as aggressively as men, that it's a two-way street. Drawing primarily on general population surveys and especially the National Family Violence Survey, which uses the controversial Conflict Tactics Scale (CTS), they claim that the causes of "domestic violence" are rooted in individual psychopathology, from alcohol abuse, mental health issues, and couples' dysfunction rather than from men's acculturation to dominate and control in relationships with women. They see the assaults as products of arguments rather than as evidence of systematic campaigns to gain and maintain control in relationships. As "gender neutral" proponents, their treatment approaches focus on the importance of seeing men and women together, addressing the psychological and addiction problems of both partners.

Critics of the CTS argue that its findings decontextualize the violence, and that it fails to take sufficiently into account the differences in strength, the intention or function of the violence, and the effects of the violence. It also doesn't address the history or pattern of the abuse, including such tactics as economic abuse, manipulation involving the children, isolation, intimidation, and threats. Another methodological flaw is that the CTS excludes incidents of violence that occur after separation and divorce, the period that has proved to be most lethal for victims of domestic violence. Think again about the growing number of women and children victims of homicide/suicides.

Dutton made quite an impression in 2004 when Families First in Atlanta invited him to present a two-day workshop on "Empirically developed treatment for intimate abuse." On the first day, he focused on mutual combatant theory, citing the CTS to make his case. Some in the audience, which comprised academics, clinicians, and advocates, respectfully critiqued his analysis, citing the failure to take into consideration the context of the violence. But it was on the second day that Dutton revealed an interesting connection between his theory and his practice.

He and Julia Perilla, then on faculty in the Department of Community Psychology at Georgia State University and the director of Caminar Latino, were on a panel to address cultural considerations in the treatment of "domestic violence." Those who were there were amazed and offended by Dutton's frequent use of interruptions and condescending and dismissive comments when responding to Julia. Julia recalls feeling shocked and insulted by his aggressive behavior. Looking back, it seems like it would have been an opportunity for men and/or women in the room to respectfully confront Dutton, labeling his behaviors, noting the effects he was having on Julia and the audience, insisting that he stop. Unfortunately, that didn't happen.

While pressures from the psychology/psychotherapy worlds have resulted in batterers' programs paying closer attention to screening and treating offenders for co-occurring conditions, including addiction and severe depression, the focus on finding mutual responsibility for the violence has resulted in whole new waves of victim-blaming and treatment modalities like couples counseling that clearly put women at greater risk.

When Men Stopping Violence first insisted that couples counseling desist when a man entered the program, I recall hearing the concerns of referring therapists who might think or even say, "Who are these people to tell me I don't know how or when to work with dysfunctional couples? And, do they really think I'm so naïve as to defer my source of revenue just because they deem my theoretical framework inappropriate?" They were offended at the prospect of having their clinical judgment questioned and their income compromised. They apparently weren't thinking about the safety and justice needs of battered women.

So that's how patriarchy works: Its gatekeeper, in this case the mental health world's providers, reframe the cause, extent and effects of men's violence to obfuscate its primary function, which is to enforce and maintain patriarchal values, systems and culture, at the expense of the oppressed, in this case battered women. And, sticking with the notion of gatekeepers, we can easily see parallel themes and strategies employed by other patriarchal institutional enforcers. Take, for example, the leaders of the "free world" (those guys in the government/ macro community section of the accountability model whom David Potter described as the Euro-American men who retreat to a room to make decisions for and about the rest of the known world) reaching out and benevolently colonizing "underdeveloped, "emerging" nations, "developing" their natural resources "for their own good" while dismantling and disrupting (with a little help from missionaries, corporate contractors, and the military) their governments, religious communities, and economies, leaving a swath of tribal warfare, economic disaster, social chaos, genocide. And, as in the case of Iraq, where, years after colonization by the British and other usual suspects, we, the United States, intervened under the benevolent guise of "stopping weapons of mass destruction" and "nation building" in order to depose a ruthless terrorist and build a "fledgling democracy." Not to mention, it seems, is our brazen intention to maintain "rightful" control of the oil reserves in the region.

It may seem a bit of a stretch to compare world leaders with psychologists, but when it comes down to who decides/frames what the problem is, what the solution is, and whom it should benefit, is it really a stretch to say that they share the similar roles and responsibilities around maintaining patriarchal interests?

CHAPTER 10

Courage and Compassion

If men could get pregnant, abortion would be a sacrament.

Florynce Kennedy

Florynce is definitely onto something here, and not just in the context of reproductive justice. Sometimes I've thought that if men could bear children we would have a shot at unraveling patriarchal culture, a culture that puts so much more emphasis on men sacrificing rather than sustaining life, on controlling rather than nurturing relationships. But since Floynce's comment is not a likely or imminent strategy for transforming the patriarchy, I'm left with contemplating more modest tactics that we know and have tried.

When I think back to and even go back to a Men Stopping Violence "Men At Work" class, I'm often struck by two things that promote healthy accountability in that room. One is the constant collective insistence that men take responsibility for their choices in their lives and in that room. Given the unfamiliar and unnatural nature of that practice, it calls for equally unusual motivating forces to sustain it. I'm thinking that one of the most powerful forces for sustaining behavioral change is men's capacity to feel empathy for the other, to move from the positions of guilting or blaming, the "other" ("other" being anyone who defies one's own version of reality, including and particularly those who have been victimized by that version) to feeling the pain from which their victim's stated truths are emanating.

When a man experiences her tears of fear, her confusion and rage, as responses to behaviors he has used rather than her attempt to shame and belittle him, he has found the ability to hear and to empathize with her experience. A capacity that is essential for the elements of justice-making and healing to take place. Kathleen once spoke of the existential crisis men experience in order to attain that capacity:

> "How to do such a thing? How does one start? How do we step outside a history, a language, and a social order that inform our every decision? One place to begin is to listen to those who have been marginalized, who have been placed outside the center of history. Women's stories, told from our own subjective reality, reveal a context in which men might start to address the real source of their dis-ease with the experience of masculinity. But this process is easier said than done, for in telling our own stories, women stop functioning as mirrors of men's centrality. Men experience this act as life-threatening; they are driven back upon themselves. The ground on which they stand and have their being is shaken. They experience an existential not-knowing. It's no surprise that they react strongly, even violently. And in that moment, they have a choice. To the men in our batterers' groups, it is then that someone says to him that he has a choice. He can either do more of what he's done—more threats, more pressure, more intimidation to put her 'in her place' or he can risk hearing her and sitting with it until

he begins to understand what a new response would be. To sit in the midst of that not-knowing bespeaks fundamental uncertainty, an untenable position for men for whom a sense of control is essential. But the batterer who transverses that time of not-knowing begins the journey toward a new life. His own personal house of cards has fallen, but he now has access to the tools to build a new house, one founded on love instead of power, freedom instead of control, liberation instead of oppression."[13]

Here Kathleen is talking about batterers, but their "journey" could apply to any of us who are in the process of redefining our relationship to patriarchy. That work includes many moments of doubt and confusion, the manifestation of which many men associate with being weak or "soft." And today, as it has long been the case, whether it's in the street, in a presidential campaign or in one of our MSV classes, to be labeled "soft" on anything might be the most damning insult you can issue another man.

When we decide to identify, elect, and appoint leaders at the Global, Macro, and Micro levels of community, who have the ability and the will to lead from perspectives rooted in compassion and empathy, there will be more opportunities for justice-making at every level of our social order. To sustain our momentum we need to remember and imagine moments when we participated in or witnessed the kind of peace and justice-making that defies and disrupts patriarchal processes. Those moments are rooted in the mundane *and* the momentous. We need only recognize and be prepared for them when they arise.

One of my earliest opportunities to witness truth speaking to power occurred during my undergraduate years in the mid-1960s. Ms. Fannie Lou Hamer, the iconic civil rights leader from Ruleville, Mississippi, came to our campus to educate students on the challenges African-Americans were facing when trying to register to vote. Challenges that included repeated beatings, death threats and other forms of lethal intimidation. What really blew my mind was that even though Ms. Hamer had experienced the most constant and humiliating forms of harassment, she was clearly unbent and convinced that she could make justice prevail. She would come into the room and, before presenting, would invite each of us to share our names and what brought us to join her that day. When she spoke, she would convey a combination of compassion and determination we'd rarely seen, punctuating her harrowing stories with inspiring sayings and songs. And I would wonder, "How could this be? How could she be mentoring us mostly white, fervent, though relatively clueless, students—sons and daughters of the same race that had brutalized her and her community?"

But there wasn't much time to reflect on that because the next thing we knew Ms. Hamer was leading a major demonstration at the 1964 Democratic National Convention. Having just founded the Mississippi Freedom Democratic Party (MFDP), she and her fellow delegates were challenging the seating of the all-white Mississippi delegation at the convention. As vice-chair of the MFDP delegation, she made an impassioned speech to the credentials committee, describing how thousands of African-Americans in Mississippi and all over the country were prevented from voting through illegal tests, taxes, and intimidation. The hearing was to be televised, but in Washington, President Lyndon Johnson, who feared that this kind of controversy would drive white southern voters into the Goldwater Republican camp, called an emergency press conference in an effort to divert press coverage from Ms. Hamer's testimony. But the networks decided to air her presentation on the late news programs, which resulted in the credentials committee receiving thousands of letters of support for the MFDP. President Johnson then dispatched Hubert Humphrey, V.P. candidate (and one of my heroes at the time) and several other powerful statesmen (including Senator Walter Mondale, Walter Reuther, United Auto Workers Union Leader, and FBI chief J. Edgar Hoover) to attempt to negotiate with the Freedom Democrats. They suggested a compromise that would give the MFDP two non-voting seats and other non-compelling concessions. But when Humphrey outlined the compromise, saying that his position on the ticket was at stake, Ms. Hamer, invoking her spiritual beliefs, sharply reprimanded him:

> "Do you mean to tell me that your position is more important than four hundred thousand black people's lives? Senator Humphrey, I know lots of people in Mississippi who have lost their jobs trying to register to vote. I had to leave the plantation where I worked in Sunflower County, Mississippi. Now if you lose this job of Vice President because you do what is right, because you help the MFDP, everything will be all right. God will take care of you. But if you take (the nomination) this way, why, you will never be able to do any good for civil rights, for poor people, for peace, or any of those things you talk about. Senator Humphrey, I'm going to pray for you."[14]

In the end the MFDP rejected the compromise but had changed the discourse to the point that the Democratic Party adopted a clause that demanded equality of representation from their states' delegations. Ms. Hamer was seated as a member of Mississippi's official delegation to the Democratic National Convention in 1968 where she was an outspoken advocate for the disenfranchised and against the war in Vietnam.

When we wonder about where and how to enter the fray on the broad spectrum of patriarchal oppression as illustrated in the "Community Accountability Model," it's useful to look to those who have been oppressed to guide us to and through those choices. Those of us who followed Ms. Hamer were provided an indelible blueprint. It remained for us to decide whether to try to live by it. Living by it calls for us to be prepared for those moments when we can further justice-making. And that preparation can resemble the work required in adopting MSVs seven aforementioned Core Principles, particularly "We Are the Work."

Another of those opportune moments occurred towards the end of my tenure at MSV. Among the hopes I held when I left the staff in 2010 was that we could find ways to become more collaborative and less competitive with our brother and sister organizations in the movement to end violence against women. While many of us (organizations) share similar if not complimentary missions, we don't always agree on how to accomplish them and we sometimes clash openly and covertly when we meet and present at national conferences and gatherings. While there's nothing particularly wrong about having these differences and disagreements, there's been too little time and effort spent learning from them and finding the common ground that can further our work.

One exception to this phenomenon has unfolded in our evolving relationship with the New York-based organization A Call to Men. Over the years MSV has collaborated with A Call to Men on federally funded train-the-trainers projects that have focused on mobilizing men to end violence against women. While I personally felt a good connection with their co-founders, Ted Bunch and Tony Porter, I'd experienced an undercurrent of tension between our organizations that I assumed was rooted in our mutual competitiveness. Who really had the best mousetrap? Who really had the word on how to do this work?

In the early stages of our joint trainings my sense was that each organization would prepare our own modules as separate and discrete presentations that would represent our respective theories and practices around why and how to mobilize men. We gave lip service if not token efforts to working collaboratively.

Then, in 2012, Men Stopping Violence partnered with A Call to Men to provide technical assistance to 13 state coalitions on how to engage men in the work to end violence against women. Customarily our MSV presentations are based on the theory and practices that have emerged from our seven Core Principles and particularly our Community Accountability Model. A Call to Men bases their work on concepts such as organizing communities to engage men in domestic and sexual violence prevention and developing tools for healthy masculinity.

Having acknowledged some inter-organizational tensions in the past, this time the training teams agreed to a more collaborative preparation process, one in which representatives from each organization would sit in on the other's planning so as to produce a more cohesive and coherent product. By all reports, being in the room together, seeing and then solving problems together, shifted the quality of the relationship in significant ways.

And then came an unexpected test for the solidarity in that relationship. As mentioned, our (MSV) trainings are based on our Core Principles and when our proposed agenda included addressing the linkage between homophobia and men's violence against women, the federal funders who approve our trainings objected to our addressing this linkage, claiming that it was not consistent with the goals of the training. I won't comment on the basis of their reasoning, nor will I say much about the devastating effect it had on our training team. But what was significant was that our trainers did include a condensed version of this point in our presentation, and then A Call to Men supported our position, standing up in the room, reinforcing the importance of understanding and acting on the principle of confronting homophobia and intersecting oppressions. It was a moment when Tony Porter and his team stood in solidarity with Ulester and our team.

I'm thinking that those are moments when to stand up for a controversial but core issue can result in jeopardizing funding for those who do so. A Call to Men could have remained silent in the room, leaving MSV to take the heat and the hit, but that didn't happen. It's not a game-changing moment. But it's a historically significant one in the sense of men overcoming patriarchal habits of control and competitiveness by listening to and empathizing with one another to further justice-making. It is another time when you know that "we are the work" is not just a saying or a slogan but a working mantra.

So maybe when we allow ourselves to know the extent and variety of patriarchal oppression we inevitably find ourselves experiencing moments that Kathleen described as "transversing the time of not knowing" of "existential uncertainty." What some men in our classes refer to as a time of spiritual crisis. Because even if we've done the preparatory work as spelled out in MSV's seven Core Principles, it takes a measure of moral strength to challenge patriarchy. At a minimum, it requires the kind of courage and compassion so clearly demonstrated by Ms. Hamer. No matter who on the patriarchal spectrum you're confronting, from the senator to the psychologist to the coach to the elders in one's own family, it calls for courage: courage to confront and courage to stay connected with those whom you're confronting. Courage to speak up and to listen, to step up and step back, to lead and to follow, to feel confusion and to stay present and not reactive in the midst of that confusion.

And it calls for compassion, for ourselves and for others. Compassion, at least for me, has been the most challenging. I've frequently looked to others to understand the meaning and the practice of compassion. Thich Nhaht Hanh, the Vietnamese Buddhist monk has been a model for me and for many regarding how compassion works. I recall hearing him describe his experience of being on the ground as American forces dropped bombs on his village. I recall him describing how he prayed for his fellow villagers, for the animals and the plants in and around the village. And then he spoke of praying for the men in the planes, for their souls so that they could heal from the trauma they would endure from inflicting great pain and suffering on others.

I remember thinking, "What is that? How could he be thinking that, feeling that, saying that, when he's under siege?" We need only think about the hundreds of thousands of returning war veterans who are suffering from post-traumatic stress syndrome, committing unthinkable destructive acts towards themselves, towards their loved ones, and towards others to know the meaning of what he said and the source of his compassion. In the words of Malcom X, it's just a classic and woeful example of "chickens coming home to roost."

My take-home message from Thay (Thich Nhat Hanh) is that compassion is the practice of staying humanely connected with the other, no matter what has transpired in that relationship. And when it comes to compassion for the self, well, to quote an oft-repeated initial response of my friend Ulester when he anticipates an especially daunting challenge: "Oh, lord." Because when we thoughtlessly engage in self-recrimination and criticism it deeply erodes our capacity to show up and be present with and for others. If we're not actively practicing loving kindness for ourselves, others will inevitably pay, and justice, let alone peace will not be served.

And so, as we consider what it looks like to take advantage of momentous and mundane opportunities to confront patriarchy, it seems fitting to return to Floryence Kennedy, who once said, while protesting the lack of female toilets at Harvard by leading a mass urination on the grounds: "I'm just a loud-mouthed, middle-aged colored lady with a fused spine and three feet of intestines missing and a lot of people think I'm crazy. Maybe you do too but I never stop to wonder why I'm not like other people. The mystery to me is why more people aren't like me."

Yup.

EPILOGUE:
We Are the Work

Not long after MSV began doing groups with batterers in the early 80s, our peers, colleagues and supporters would say things like, "Hey, it's great that you're working with men, but when are you going to work with boys so that you can get catch the problem before it's too late?" And we would say something like, "You're right. It's important to work with boys and it's our belief that boys are watching and learning from the primary men in their lives, including their fathers, brothers, coaches, assistant principals, and employers. Men in their lived lives who on a day-to-day basis have the opportunity to model what it means to be responsible and accountable in their relationships with women, children, and other men."

It's not that focusing on men is more important than focusing on boys. It's that to try to do both would result in our doing neither adequately. Our focus and our resources would be scattered and depleted. So, we established our work with men as our niche. And while initially the men we focused on were men who got "caught" for abusing women, our work eventually evolved into reaching out to and engaging with all men. As mentioned earlier, we have partnered with the Office on Violence Against Women, A Call to Men, Futures Without Violence and others to promote that work. But when inviting individual men and entire organizations to focus on mobilizing men, it calls to question: What does it take to prepare men to do this work? Is it a matter of acquiring a particular body of knowledge and set of skills to facilitate men's participation in mobilizing men? And how do you know what those requisite knowledge and skills are and where to apply them? As a way to answer that question, I want to digress to an update on MSV's history.

When Eesha Pandit became MSV's fourth executive director in the latter part of 2012, it was fitting that she came from a background of working in the human and reproductive rights movements. While she was clearly versed in the work of addressing sexual and domestic violence, she brought with her a vision and analysis that broadened the spectrum of that work. Her experience, personally and vocationally, led her to identify and address the interconnections between poverty, racism, sexism, heterosexism, and xenophobia, not as add-ons to the work of ending violence against women, but as the work itself. She could readily see how the "silo" mentality of addressing each issue separately and individually was costly to the full spectrum of women who are affected by patriarchal violence. Compartmentalizing the issues was to compartmentalize women and to profoundly limit and dilute our strategies for addressing their oppression.

One place I experienced compartmentalizing, if not competitiveness among and by advocates, was during the lobbying process at the Georgia state legislative session. I can remember preparing to go to the capitol to educate legislators on bills specifically addressing domestic violence, hearing implicit and sometimes explicit messages not to confuse our representatives or compromise our efforts by speaking up or drawing links between domestic violence and reproductive rights. And, in the more distant past, it was considered questionable if not literally costly (since state funding for rape crisis centers might dilute funding for domestic violence programs) to advocate for bills addressing sexual assault (SA) and bills addressing domestic violence (DV). While the DV and SA worlds have made significant progress in collaborating and supporting each other nationally, I still believe that in Georgia the SA world is seen as the "little sister" to the DV world. And in my mind it triggers, among other contradictions, thoughts about the growing number of men I've interviewed for the 24-week program who, when I asked what they do or have done when their partners decline sex, admit to committing the statutory definition of rape. (It was as recent as 1993 that marital rape became a criminal offense in all 50 states.)

And then there was the 2012 Georgia legislative session when a majority of Georgia legislators were promoting an oppressive and restrictive immigration law, which opponents in Georgia and across the country have criticized for its "racial profiling." Advocates for immigrant battered women in Georgia were struggling to voice the predicaments this legislation would present for battered immigrant women and receiving what I considered to be reticent support from their DV allies. To the degree that it was true, there may have been several explanations, but I know that I was speculating that it was because of the concern that providing vocal and visible support for immigrant women would be perceived as challenging the illegal immigration bill and ultimately jeopardize support for the domestic violence legislative package.

These are moments when issues such as reproductive rights, sexual assault, domestic violence and immigration reform are seen and treated as separate and not equal.

So Eesha came to MSV to join and galvanize the position that MSV rejects the compartmentalizing of these issues because of how it negatively affects women and because of how it compromises the effectiveness of our work. And so her arrival also coincided with the refining of the way we define our niche, which brings us back to the question regarding what is MSV's role in preparing individuals and organizations to mobilize men.

As I write this, MSV is in the pilot stage of a training that prepares men and women to do the work of mobilizing communities to end VAW. What seems unique about this training and how it speaks to MSV's evolving niche is the importance it places on individuals and organizations acquiring a cultural competence to do the work. MSV has historically provided skills-based ("nuts and bolts") trainings on how to work with men, how men can work with women, mentor boys, engage with daughters, but the Mobilizing Men to Prevent Violence Against Women training invites participants to explore the cultural and historical context of our work and the social justice movements that are at the root of our work as a way to determine where we stand personally and organizationally. The previous example of how divided we became at the legislature around issues of immigration, choice, and sexual assault suggest that too many of us in the domestic violence and sexual assault movement are lacking an understanding of how these and other related issues are connected. I don't believe that those choices were made out of malevolence or bad intentions. They came from fear (of loss of funding) and lack of understanding (i.e. battered women are also immigrant women, also rape victims, also women entitled to reproductive choices). A fundamental tenet of patriarchal violence is to create a climate of scarcity, pitching one oppressed group against another, encouraging competition for limited resources, and reducing their options by dividing constituents who are actually natural allies.

So, if we are to effectively address violence against *all* women, we have to understand the socio-political necessity of addressing poverty, racism, housing, health, homelessness, heterosexism, ableism—you know the drill. This training challenges participants to understand their position on each of these issues: where their interests, biases, strengths and liabilities lie. It is one thing to understand the dynamics of patriarchal violence through the lens of the Community-Accountability Model. It is quite another to strategically plan for where and when and how you and or your organization will choose to resist those forces. This training represents the culmination of MSV's movement from theory to practice, from placing the principle "Intersectionality Matters" in a prominent place in our analysis to facilitating action plans for how to do it. This training, then, provides the ultimate experience of practicing the principle "We Are the Work," starting with the self to identify and address those blind spots that may interfere with one's capacity for justice-making.

When I think of how to implement the other Core Principles, it always seems to start with "We Are the Work," because whether you're dealing with an individual batterer, a judge, legislator, or the systems that produce them, you will need to know how cultural and historical context, yours and theirs, informs how you will engage.

So no matter who, where, and when it is, we are the work.

APPENDIX A:
The Core Principles

The work of Men Stopping Violence (MSV) is supported by its seven Core Principles, which have been developed, reviewed and refined over three decades of working to end violence against women.

1. Women's voices and experiences must be central to our work with men.

If we are to hear important truths about male violence against women and how it affects us, we must seek out women's voices and experiences. But which women? Not all women are in agreement on issues regarding gender-based violence. Also, men do not have to agree with everything women express, but to be effective in ending violence against women, they must be willing to hear and see the experiences of women across divisions of class, ethnicity, race and sexual orientation. Women are not only experts on their own lives but on the lives of men as well, since the threat of male violence requires them to study men closely in order to stay safe. Men can learn about women's experiences by reading, by embracing their artistic expressions, and, when we are willing, by listening to women's voices.

2. Race matters.

Although race is a social construct, it has meaning for how we are treated, how we treat others, and how we view ourselves. Our society, influenced by the concept of race, is organized in a hierarchical social structure that situates whites at its apex. This hierarchical social structure fosters the oppression of communities of color and reinforces the daily tensions and conflicts between whites and people of color. Also, it creates complex power struggles within communities of color as they work to resist the *divide-and-conquer* traps. When working to end male violence against women, it is important to remember that the history of women of color and the history of white women are not parallel. Strategies that work for white women may not work for women of color. Although the battered women's movement involves all races and classes, the white middle-class narrative has usually dominated.

3. Intersectionality (gender, class, and sexual orientation) matters.

All forms of oppression are interconnected. *Intersectionality* speaks to the relationship between oppressions, including those based on race, gender, class, and sexual orientation. Intersectionality can be a difficult concept to put into practice because of our training, and sometimes desire, to be single-issue-focused. For example, when addressing male violence against women, we tend to focus almost exclusively on gender at the expense of race. Each oppression reinforces the others, and therefore, attempts to create a hierarchy of oppression will prove futile. An example of how we might practice intersectionality is, that when we make decisions, whether policy, research, funding, etc., we filter them through the prism of class, race, sexual orientation, gender, etc. In other words ask, "What are the class, race, sexual orientation and gender considerations and implications of my actions?" Addressing intersectionality in our work will make us more effective in responding to the needs of victims and holding perpetrators accountable.

4. Community accountability is key to ending violence against women.

Holding men accountable for their violence is an essential prerequisite for pursuing safety and justice for women. Currently, we rely primarily on the criminal-legal system to arrest, prosecute, and impose consequences on perpetrators. However, the criminal-legal system can be problematic for many women because it frequently imposes consequences on him that do not work for her. For example, arrest and jail may result in his lost employment, thereby producing economic and safety challenges for her. For accountability to work for victims, we must grow the number of community partners and institutions that send a clear message that violence against women is unacceptable and that when a man in that community abuses a woman, he will experience swift and meaningful consequences. Key community partners, such as faith-based communities and businesses, can set policies and procedures that will impose limits and consequences for offenders while providing opportunities for safety and empowerment for victims. In doing so, we aren't reducing the role of the criminal legal system; rather, we are expanding the number of community gatekeepers and stakeholders who can cooperatively work to promote community accountability.

5. Organizing men to end violence takes precedence over intervening with batterers.

Although well-intentioned, the emphasis on rehabilitating batterers is shortsighted, and has done little to transform the culture of violence against women. Only a small percentage of abusive, violent men enter intervention programs, and the jury is still out about the effectiveness of these programs in creating safety for women. And even if every man who completes an intervention program succeeds in stopping his abusive behaviors, there would be little change to community norms that reward men for sexist, abusive, and violent behaviors. It is often difficult for some men to see how their beliefs, actions, or inactions might condone violence against women. A man may think, for example, that if he witnesses a man abusing a woman, it is inappropriate to interfere. By mobilizing *all* men to prevent violence against women, we stand a better chance of ending violence against women.

6. We are the work.

To change the world, we must become aware of how we move within it. For example, we need to be conscious of how we use our power. Thus, organizing for change begins with examining our part in maintaining and undoing social inequities. When we see how we are part of the problem, we can make an informed decision to be part of the solution. Without this kind of self-examination, we are likely to deny and minimize our abusive behaviors, as well as others'. We must make the connection between ourselves and the culture of violence by drawing on our own experiences—as victims and as perpetrators. This work is ongoing, and it better prepares us to challenge individuals and institutions that promote violence against women.

7. Patriarchal violence must be addressed.

Violence against women cannot be fully addressed without understanding patriarchy, which author and scholar bell hooks describes as

> "a political-social system that insists that male are inherently dominating, superior to everything and anyone deemed weak, especially females, and endowed

with the right to dominate and rule over the weak and
to maintain that dominance through various forms of
psychological terrorism and violence."

Patriarchal violence, which includes domestic and sexual violence, is used to maintain that system. Patriarchy also requires that boys and men adhere to codes of masculinity that are self-destructive and destructive to others. The overwhelming majority of domestic and sexual violence victims are women and the overwhelming perpetrators of that violence are men. Until we as a culture acknowledge that violent men are operating within a system that condones and encourages their violence, we will not end male violence against women.

APPENDIX B:
The Core Values of Because We Have Daughters®

All games, activities discussions in BWHD are based on a set of Core Values.

1. **Listening.** So often, instead of listening to what is being said to us, we are mentally preparing our response. Really listening is a skill that takes patient practice, but the rewards are enormous. Many times our daughters would rather we heard their story than grant their request. Listening is a sign of respect. It demonstrates that we value the speaker. We believe that listening is the most important thing we can do in Because We Have Daughters˚.

2. **Equitable and shared decision-making.** The process of sharing ideas in a respectful way is as important as resolving a situation. In interactions with their daughters, fathers are used to coming up with "the answer" to a challenge or conflict, but allowing open discussion leaves space for girls to explore their own ideas with confidence.

3. **Awareness of space.** Fathers are encouraged to pause in different situations to allow time and space for their daughters. This pausing applies to different situations, such as pausing in a conversation to hear another point of view or pausing during an activity to ensure that everyone feels included. BWHD

activities build awareness of the need to provide space for girls to expand to their full personhood.

4. **Assertiveness.** Communicating wants and needs is important for both fathers and daughters. In BWHD, everyone has opportunities to practice assertiveness and to practice without being aggressive or manipulating.

5. **Appreciation for non-traditional qualities.** Fathers can encourage daughters to explore a full range of possibilities for their lives by expressing appreciation for nontraditional qualities daughters might possess.

6. **Discussing difficult issues without judgment.** Being able to talk about difficult issues without blaming, minimizing, or judging can help bridge the traditional divide between men and women. Fathers who learn to listen actively and suspend judgment can strengthen their relationships with their daughters.

7. **Awareness and understanding of societal pressures girls and women face.** All girls and women live with the knowledge that they could be assaulted by someone they know or even love. BWHD provides an opportunity for men to learn what it is like to live with that knowledge and how it shapes a women's reality.

APPENDIX C:
How BWHD works

The general format of the program calls for gatherings of groups of fathers and daughters. These gatherings last approximately three hours and consist of fun activities that dads and daughters participate in together, as well as discussion groups for both dads and daughters that allow an exploration of any insights that grew out of these activities.

There are four basic types of BWHD activities:

- **Task-oriented**
- **Performance-based**
- **Physical**
- **Arts and crafts**

Task-oriented activities engage dads and daughters in completing a project together. Facilitators will need to make sure that the groups stay on task in order to finish in the allotted time. Task-oriented activities provide a particularly good opportunity to focus on the Core Value of equitable and shared decision-making. The goal is not to complete the task. It is to provide a way for all the participants to offer suggestions as to how the activity will be accomplished. Our experience is that dads really like task-oriented activities, so they are a good way to get fathers engaged in BWHD.

Performance-based activities are good when there is a smaller number of participants. Often this type of activity is a way for dads to experience the Core Value of appreciation for non-traditional qualities. A daughter may decide that she wants to perform as a racecar driver or pirate. Also, we have found that performance activities provide a way for younger daughters to shine, because they are more comfortable with make-believe than the dads or older daughters.

Next, there are the **physical activities**. Facilitators can use this type of activity to familiarize participants with the Core Value awareness of space by encouraging the fathers to pause in different situations to allow time and space for their daughters. It can be challenging to come up with activities that don't have a "winner"; however, it is up to the facilitators to ensure that the activities are non-competitive.

Arts and crafts activities give the girls and dads an opportunity to be creative. With these activities dad gets to see what kind of imagination his daughter has. They also give dad a way to get in touch with his own imagination.

Beyond the session

To help meet the overall goal of BWHD, which is to create safer communities for women and children, we hope that participants will internalize the tools and education they gain in the program and share it in their communities. The idea is that dads will begin to have conversations with the men in their lives (family, friends, co-workers, congregation members) that they have never had before. Our hope is that dads will become aware that the conversations they have can either perpetuate or challenge violence against women. Men oftentimes have conversations that reinforce negative opinions about women. BWHD provides opportunities for a dad to see that the ways in which he views women and talks about women contribute to the overall societal view of women and girls that ultimately affects his daughter.

Our hope is that men will see how objectifying women does not create a safe environment for their daughters. They can begin to explain to other men that objectification means just that—turning women into objects, like body parts. When girls and women are objects, they are not people, so violence against them is much easier to commit. BWHD helps men learn to challenge other men in a constructive manner that doesn't shame them, allowing them to receive education without feeling judged.

Challenging standard societal gender roles is a powerful way to create a sense of self for daughters attending BWHD. Girls often feel as though they have to conform to what society says a girl should be, look like, or act like. In BWHD, daughters have opportunities to express themselves without being punished for not conforming to restrictive roles.

Such rigid gender roles also affect men negatively. Men are taught that they can't ask for help, they need to have the answer, must be strong and unemotional (except for getting angry), and in control. BWHD provides men with an alternative view of what it means to be a man. They can ask for help, have conversations to arrive at an answer, feel sad or scared, and share decision-making with others. We have found that when we give men a safe space to explore a different definition of masculinity, many feel relieved and excited by the possibility of doing things differently.

APPENDIX D:
The Men Stopping Violence
Community-Accountability Model

The MSV community-accountability model identifies patriarchy as the root cause of violence against women. It illustrates how that sociopolitical system instructs individuals at different levels of community to enforce and reinforce messages of male supremacy. The MSV model is not used to predict individual violent behavior by identifying risk factors. It is used to identify the socializing messages and behaviors that create a climate of violence so that responses can be crafted that advocate individual responsibility while looking beyond the individual to encourage cultural change.

MSV's ecological model is organized around the different levels of influence at which patriarchy asserts itself and identifies those levels at which patriarchal norms can be disrupted. The MSV community-accountability model names the function of each level and focuses on the messages conveyed by each community represented. How these communities interconnect and how those patriarchal messages are interpreted, acted upon, and redeployed throughout the system of communities is vital to understanding how individual men are influenced and how, in turn, they influence the communities of which they are a part. So although MSV acknowledges the need for individual responsibility, the organization also recognizes that communities are responsible for addressing the messages and policies that create the climate in which violence against women occurs.

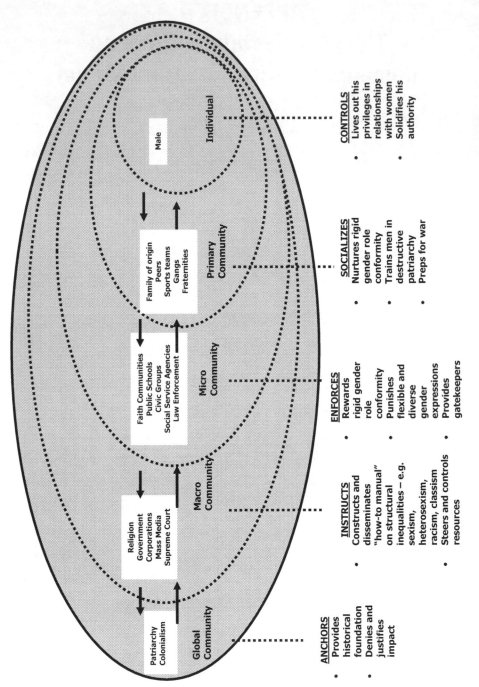

The Men Stopping Violence Community-Accountability Model of Male Violence Against Women © 2007 Men Stopping Violence, Inc.

ENDNOTES

1. Carlin, Kathleen. "Working with Batterers: What is Women's Role?" Men Stopping Violence. http://www.menstoppingviolence.org. Website archives: June 10, 2011.
2. Ibid.
3. Ibid.
4. Carlin, Kathleen. Speech presentation at Special Institute of the National Coalition Against Domestic Violence, National Conference, 1982. Men Stopping Violence. http://www.menstoppingviolence.org. Website archives: July 15, 2013.
5. Ibid.
6. Ibid.
7. Carlin, Kathleen. "Measuring Success," in *Uptake*: Men Stopping Violence newsletter, No. 5, 1996.
8. Perilla, Julia and Felipe Perez. "A Program for Immigrant Latino Men Who Batter Within the Context of a Comprehensive Family Intervention," in *Programs for Men Who Batter*, edited by Etiony Aldarondo and Fernando Mederos. Civic Research Institute, 2003, 11-3.
9. Ibid.
10. Crenshaw, Kimberle. "Mapping the Margins: Intersectionality, Identity Politics and Violence Against Women of Color," in *Stanford Law Review*, Vol. 43, July 1991.
11. hooks, bell. *The Will to Change: Men, Masculinity and Love*. Atria Publishing, New York: 2003.
12. Douglas, Ulester, Dick Bathrick and Phyllis Alesia Perry. "Deconstructing Male Violence Against Women, The Men Stopping Violence Community Accountability Model," in *Violence Against Women*, 14:2, February 2008.
13. Carlin, Kathleen. "Men's Movement of Choice," in *Women Respond to the Men's Movement*, edited by Kay Leigh Hagan. Pandora Press, London: 1992.
14. "Fannie Lou Hamer." *Wikipedia: The Free Encyclopedia*. Wikimedia Foundation, Inc. 24 June 2013. Web.

ABOUT THE AUTHOR

Born of the social justice movements of the 60s, Dick Bathrick draws on 50 years as an activist, as co-founder of Men Stopping Violence, and as skilled raconteur, to recount the compelling story of how MSV first came to be, and then came to achieve international acclaim in the movement to end men's violence against women.